Oral Workshop

新编英语口语教程 初级

主 编　吴祯福

副主编　夏玉和

编 者　李又文　王一虹　夏玉和

外语教学与研究出版社

FOREIGN LANGUAGE TEACHING AND RESEARCH PRESS

北京 BEIJING

图书在版编目（CIP）数据

新编英语口语教程. 初级 / 吴祯福主编；李又文，王一虹，夏玉和编. -- 北京：外语教学与研究出版社，2023.7
ISBN 978-7-5213-4700-5

I. ①新… II. ①吴… ②李… ③王… ④夏… III. ①英语－口语－教材 IV. ①H319.9

中国国家版本馆 CIP 数据核字 (2023) 第 135216 号

出 版 人　王　芳
项目负责　孙蒲富阳
责任编辑　李丹丹
责任校对　曹　妮
封面设计　梧桐影
版式设计　付玉梅
出版发行　外语教学与研究出版社
社　　址　北京市西三环北路 19 号（100089）
网　　址　https://www.fltrp.com
印　　刷　三河市紫恒印装有限公司
开　　本　787×1092　1/16
印　　张　16
版　　次　2023 年 11 月第 1 版　2023 年 11 月第 1 次印刷
书　　号　ISBN 978-7-5213-4700-5
定　　价　55.90 元

如有图书采购需求，图书内容或印刷装订等问题，侵权、盗版书籍等线索，请拨打以下电话或关注官方服务号：
客服电话：400 898 7008
官方服务号：微信搜索并关注公众号"外研社官方服务号"
外研社购书网址：https://fltrp.tmall.com

物料号：347000001

前 言

　　倾听与表达是口语交流的两个重要方面。倾听是高水平口语交流的前提，清晰、精准、恰当的表达是高效交流的基本要求。我们的口语教材致力于培养中国学生的口头交际能力，在基础阶段教师必须帮助学生养成良好的口头交际习惯：清晰、流畅、达意；培养学生用简单而基本正确的英语表达思想的能力，同时提升学生的思维能力和逻辑能力。根据这样的训练目标，我们选择的课文文体既不过于正式，又不过于松散，课文的语言基本上属于常规语言。

　　语言是一项技能，没有大量的实践，准确而熟练地掌握英语是不可能的。有些中国学生因为缺乏英语学习环境，用英语进行口头交际的能力偏弱。学生对口语有惧怕感，突破不了口语关。为了寻找一种鼓励学生用英语进行口头交际的办法，我们通过试验与探索，研究国内外的口语教材以及中国学生学习英语口语的特定环境，评估《英语口语教程》在过往 30 年的使用情况，对此教材进行了较大范围的修订。

　　《英语口语教程》由北京外国语大学吴祯福教授主持编写，自问世以来，已经累计销售数百万册，曾经成为国内主要高等学校英语专业的指定口语教材，哺育了一届又一届的英语学习者。我们希望这套教材能继续发挥优秀教材的特色，在提高学生认知水平和培养能力等方面达到新的高度。因此，我们对《英语口语教程》进行了修订，出版《新编英语口语教程》。

　　《新编英语口语教程》分初级、中级、高级三册，训练重点不同、内容各异。此套教材根据选篇设计了多种练习，从机械训练开始，过渡到半机械训练，最后达到自由交际的目的。我们认为，任何简单的语言都可以教活，任何简单的口语训练最终都可以，也应该与"交际"联系在一起。

　　需要强调的是：在口语课上学生应是积极主动的参与者，教师只起到引导的作用。教师应最大限度地为学生提供语言实践的机会，加大学生的口头实践量。在训练过程中，教师应严格要求语言的准确、流畅。同时，在交际和运用中，教师应更多地鼓励学生积极思考，交流看法；对于学生语言错误的纠正应置于第二位，纠正语言错误宜在交际暂告一段时进行，以避免打断学生的思路和语流。

《新编英语口语教程》在保留原有教材特点的同时，更加关注学生口语学习过程，如：

1) 课文主题与学生生活、思想紧密相关，题材广泛，有助于学生产生用英语进行口头交际的强烈欲望；

2) 注重学生口语学习过程中倾听能力的培养，强调听力领先，培养学生听语篇、听语意、猜词的能力；

3) 依照任务型教学活动设计思路，精心设计练习，形式活泼多样，训练由易到难、循序渐进，练习方法多是我们在教学中多年来反复使用、卓有成效的；

4) 以培养学生语言交流能力为最终教学目标，最大限度地挖掘现有课文素材，培养学生的综合口语能力，包括叙述、对话、交谈、辩论等多种能力；

5) 教材适用性强，既适合在校的不同年级的学生，也适用于同等水平的英语自学者；

6) 每册教材都配有英语音频，声音清晰、流畅、优美，语音、语调标准纯正。

《新编英语口语教程》（初级）内容包括饮食起居、生日聚会、作客、电视、电影、购物、求医、旅游等。课文多是与日常生活相关的小故事与对话。本册教学重点是训练叙事的技能。这一训练将有利于提高学生成段说话的能力。训练从复述开始，好的复述应该是：忠实于原文内容，保留重要情节，舍去非实质性的细节；复述者应根据自己的思维重新建构，用自己的语言进行表达。

研究并遵循学生的学习规律尤为重要，因为只有遵循学生学的规律，教的方法才是科学的。《新编英语口语教程》将有助于我们和一线教师共同精进英语口语教学。

我们将此书献给辛勤耕耘的英语老师，献给求知若渴的英语学习者。

本书如有疏漏与不妥之处，敬请批评指正。

编者

于北京外国语大学

Contents

Lesson 1   Text A   There Is Something Very Nice Inside Your Drum. 1

Text B   May I See a Hat, Please? 2

Text C   Did You Enjoy Last Night's TV Program? 5

Lesson 2   Text A   But the Chinese Did! 8

Text B   At the Birthday Party 9

Text C   The Self-service 11

Lesson 3   Text A   My Dishwasher 15

Text B   Summer Plans 16

Text C   Who Waits for Whom? 18

Lesson 4   Text A   After a Heavy Snowstorm 22

Text B   No Baseball Today. 24

Text C   An Accident 26

Lesson 5   Text A   Stop Eating Fried Potatoes. 29

Text B   Keep Him in Bed. 31

Text C   The Man with a Black Bag 33

Lesson 6   Text A   A Beautiful Dress 37

Text B   Which Bus Shall I Take? 39

Text C   Volunteer in the Fight Against Desertification. 41

Lesson 7   Text A   A Visit to Conwy Castle 45

Text B   New Year's Resolutions 46

Text C   A Busy Afternoon 49

Lesson 8	Text A	A Tall and Slim Girl	52
	Text B	What a Mess!	53
	Text C	Better Be a Stupid Man.	55
Lesson 9	Text A	You Are Too Young to Buy Alcohol.	59
	Text B	Give Me a Big Box of Chocolates.	60
	Text C	An Artist and a Farmer	63
Lesson 10	Text A	They Don't Talk.	67
	Text B	A Dirty Car	69
	Text C	The Garden Work	71
Lesson 11	Text A	I'll Start in Three Months' Time.	74
	Text B	I'll Find My Way.	76
	Text C	A Break in the Routine	78
Lesson 12	Text A	The Charcoal Pit	83
	Text B	There Is Hope for Us!	84
	Text C	The Snow in the Morning	86
Lesson 13	Text A	The Country Schoolhouse	90
	Text B	On a Camping Holiday	92
	Text C	A Depressing Film	94
Lesson 14	Text A	What's Going On Here?	98
	Text B	A Lesson to Learn	99
	Text C	A Pair of Stilts	101
Lesson 15	Text A	The Honesty	105
	Text B	A Difficult Language to Learn	107
	Text C	They Are Here in My Hand!	109
Lesson 16	Text A	The Cellphone Rang Again!	113
	Text B	Bill Is Very Rude!	115
	Text C	Billy's Motorcycle Was Stolen.	117

Lesson 17 Text A The Stolen Smells...121

　　　　　Text B What Do the Romans Do?.......................................123

　　　　　Text C Mrs. Smith Meets Mrs. Turnbull. 125

Lesson 18 Text A How to Make Everybody Happy?................................130

　　　　　Text B What Do You Do After Work?...................................131

　　　　　Text C Going to the Theater..134

Lesson 19 Text A A One-hundred-dollar Bill.......................................138

　　　　　Text B A Babysitter...140

　　　　　Text C Miss Green Goes On a Diet. 142

Lesson 20 Text A What Are the Times of Meals? 146

　　　　　Text B The Food Is Bad. 148

　　　　　Text C What Would You Like to Do Tonight? 150

Lesson 21 Text A Under a Terrible Strain..154

　　　　　Text B The Shopping List 156

　　　　　Text C A Language Mix-up 158

Lesson 22 Text A Some Sausage Sandwiches.......................................162

　　　　　Text B Which of the Two Is Better?.....................................164

　　　　　Text C I'll Have One Handy. 166

Lesson 23 Text A The Bloody Thumb...170

　　　　　Text B The Party 172

　　　　　Text C How Did You Lose Your Way?..................................174

Lesson 24 Text A We Are Not Deaf!..179

　　　　　Text B That Hurts a Lot. 181

　　　　　Text C At the Doctor's 183

Lesson 25 Text A A Pocketful of Pigs...188

　　　　　Text B Let's Play Chess. 189

　　　　　Text C Can I Get My Money Back? 191

Lesson 26　Text A　The Stage Fright 195

　　　　　　Text B　I Shall Never Fly Again. 197

　　　　　　Text C　Never Give Up! 199

Lesson 27　Text A　They Threatened Me with a Knife. 204

　　　　　　Text B　Three Wishes 205

　　　　　　Text C　My Uncle 208

Lesson 28　Text A　Do You Know Who I Am? 215

　　　　　　Text B　Hands Up! 217

　　　　　　Text C　Henry's Life 219

Lesson 29　Text A　My Father's Son 226

　　　　　　Text B　What's the Matter with You? 228

　　　　　　Text C　A Miserly Master and a Greedy Servant 230

Lesson 30　Text A　Learn to Eat like a Grown-up. 237

　　　　　　Text B　A Quiz on General Knowledge 239

　　　　　　Text C　Good Manners 241

Lesson 1

Text A

There Is Something Very Nice Inside Your Drum.

1 **Discuss briefly the questions with your partner.**

Did you get birthday presents when you were a child? Which one did you like best? Why?

2 **Listen to Text A once and answer the following questions.**

1 What is the story about?

_____

2 Who liked the drum best? Who hated the drum?

_____

3 What do you think happened to the drum in the end?

_____

3 **Listen to Text A again. Take notes and answer the questions below.**

1 How old was Jimmy?

_____

2 What did Jimmy receive on his birthday?

_____

3 What did his father say when he saw the beautiful drum?

_____

4 What did his mother say in reply?

_____

5 What did Jimmy do with the drum?

_____

6 Did his parents say anything when Jimmy hit the drum?

_____

7   Did Jimmy's neighbors like his drum? Why?

_____

8   What did one of Jimmy's neighbors do a few days later?

_____

4 **Retell the story of Text A.**

1   Form a group of three or four and retell the story together. Take turns to give sentences until the story is completed. You may choose one of the following examples as the beginning of your story.

> • Last month, my son, Jimmy, had his fifth birthday. My father and other family members gave him a lot of gifts. The one he liked very much was...
> • On my fifth birthday, my grandpa bought me a beautiful big drum. I liked it very much...
> • My neighbor has a five-year-old son called Jimmy. He is so cute that...

2   Regroup with students from different groups in step 1. Each student retells the story from his/her previous group.

5 **Discuss the following questions in groups of three or four. After the discussion, select one member of your group to report to the class what you have talked about.**

1   What kind of birthday presents do you want to buy for your parents? Why?
2   Should we spend a lot of money on presents? What is your view? Why?
3   How would you like to end the story?

Text B

May I See a Hat, Please?

1 **Listen to Text B once and answer the following questions.**

1   Where does the conversation take place?

_____

2   What is the relationship between the two?

_____

3   Is it a deal?

_____

2 **Listen to Text B again. Take notes and answer the questions below.**

1   What does Mr. Ross want to buy?

_____

2   What does the salesman want to know about Mr. Ross?

_____

3   Mr. Ross does not know the size he wears, does he?

_____

4   How does the salesman get to know Mr. Ross' size?

_____

5   What color of hat does Mr. Ross prefer?

_____

6   How much is the hat?

_____

7   How does the salesman pack the hat?

_____

3 **Describe to your partner the picture below with the following words and expressions.**

a hat shop
a department store
a hat counter
by the counter
a customer who needs to buy a hat

in suits
wear a tie
a pair of big spectacles
try on a hat
fit him nicely
take size X
a favorite color
try/show different kinds of nice hats
a hard-felt hat
with a dark hat band
look in a mirror on the counter
fit well
match sth.
a good match
be satisfied with
the price of the hat
a salesman
in a dark suit
stand behind
look at the man trying on the hat
look very pleased

4 **Suppose you are Mr. Ross and your partner is the salesperson. With his/her help, you find the hat you want, but you want to buy it at a lower price. Bargain with your partner.**

Text C

Did You Enjoy Last Night's TV Program?

1 **Play the audio of the following text to your partner. Your partner listens without looking at the text.**

Frank and Charles discuss last night's television program.

Frank: Did you watch television last night, Charles?
Charles: Yes, I did.
Frank: It was a good game, wasn't it?
Charles: Oh, I didn't watch the football match. I wanted to, but my wife preferred to see the old film.
Frank: What a pity! It was quite exciting. Both teams played very well.
Charles: How did it finish?
Frank: It finished in a draw. What was the film like?
Charles: It was quite good. But I missed the beginning of it because I had to eat first.
Frank: Did your wife enjoy it?
Charles: No, she didn't. After half an hour, she stopped watching and started to read a book.

2 **Your partner retells what the conversation is about. Check if any information is missing in his/her retelling.**

3 **Ask your partner if he/she likes to watch sports programs on TV or live in the stadium. Ask him/her to explain why. You can also share your answers with your partner.**

Sentence-making

Pick out useful words and expressions from the following sentences and make sentences with them.

Example

He **made** a terrible **noise with** it.

> Stop making any noise with your chair.

- There is something very nice inside your drum.
- What size do you take?
- Try this hat on.
- I like this one. It goes very well with my coat.
- I wanted to, but my wife preferred to see the old film.
- But I missed the beginning of it because I had to eat first.

Scripts

Text A   There Is Something Very Nice Inside Your Drum[1].

It was Jimmy's birthday, and he was five years old. He got quite a lot of[2] nice birthday presents from his family, and one of them was a beautiful big drum[3].

"Who gave him that thing?" Jimmy's father said when he saw it.

"His grandfather did[4]," answered Jimmy's mother.

"Oh," said his father.

Of course, Jimmy liked his drum very much. He made a terrible noise with it, but his mother did not mind. His father was working during the day, and Jimmy was in bed when he got home in the evening, so he did not hear the noise.

But one of the neighbors did not like the noise at all[5], so one morning a few days later, she took a sharp knife and went to Jimmy's house while he was hitting his drum[6]. She said to him, "Hello, Jimmy. Do you know there's something very nice inside your drum? Here's a knife. Open the drum and let's find it."

Text B   May I See a Hat, Please?

Mr. Ross: May I see a hat, please?

Salesman: What size do you take?[7]

Mr. Ross: I'm sorry. I don't know.

Salesman: I'll measure you.[8] You take size six. What color of hat would you like?

Mr. Ross: Brown, please.

Salesman: Here are some nice brown hats. Try this hat on. It's a very good one.

Mr. Ross: Yes, I like this one. It goes very well with my coat.[9] How much is it?

Salesman: It's $9.95 (nine dollars and ninety-five cents). Do you want me to put it in a box?

Notes

1   Inside Your Drum: 在你的鼓里

2   quite a lot of: 许多，相当多

3   one of them was a beautiful big drum: 其中有一件是个好看的大鼓

4   His grandfather did: 他的祖父送的

5   not...at all: 一点也不

6   while he was hitting his drum: 当他在敲鼓时

7   What size do you take?: 您戴几号的（帽子）？

8   I'll measure you.: 我给您量一下。

9   It goes very well with my coat.: 这一顶与我的大衣十分相配。

Lesson 2

Text A

But the Chinese Did!

1 **Discuss briefly the questions with your partner.**

Have you traveled to any foreign countries before? Or have you been to a place where you don't understand the local dialect? Share your experience.

2 **Listen to Text A once and answer the following questions.**

1   Who are the people in the conversation?

2   What are they talking about?

3 **Listen to Text A again. Take notes and answer the questions below.**

1   Does Tom speak Chinese or not?

2   What did he do before he left for China?

3   How long did he study Chinese?

4   He studied hard, didn't he?

5   How long did Tom stay in China?

6   Did he have any trouble with his Chinese while he was in China?

7   What is the meaning of Tom's last sentence?

4 **Retell the story of Text A.**

1 Form a group of three or four and retell the story together. Take turns to give sentences until the story is completed. You may choose one of the following examples as the beginning of your story.

- One day, I went to China for a holiday.
- My friend, Tom, visited China one day.

2 Regroup with students from different groups in step 1. Each student retells the story from his/her previous group.

5 **Discuss the following questions in groups of three or four. After the discussion, select one member of your group to report to the class what you have talked about.**

1 Do you like traveling? What do you like about traveling?
2 Do you prefer to travel to one place and stay there long enough, or do you prefer to travel to different places on one trip? Why?

Text B

At the Birthday Party

1 **Listen to Text B once and answer the following questions.**

1 Where did the conversations take place?

_____

2 Who were the people in the conversations?

_____

3 What was Mrs. Ross doing at home?

_____

4 Where were the boys and girls?

_____

5 What were they doing there?

_____

2 **Listen to Text B again. Take notes and answer the questions below.**

1   Who came late? Why was he late?

_____

2   What did John tell Peter?

_____

3   What did Peter say when he saw Alice?

_____

4   What did Alice ask Peter to do?

_____

5   What was Alice going to do?

_____

6   Who did Peter notice when he was in the dining room?

_____

7   How did Peter learn the girl's name?

_____

8   What did John ask Peter to do?

_____

9   Did Peter invite Joan for a dance?

_____

10 Did Joan accept Peter's invitation?

_____

3 **Describe to your partner the picture below with the following words and expressions.**

hold a (birthday) party for sb.

a hostess

friends and classmates

in suits

in beautiful skirts

birthday presents

a birthday cake

a dancing partner

nice and beautiful music

dance to the music

dance beautifully/gracefully

enjoy themselves

cut the cake

have her (fourteenth) birthday

4 Suppose your partner is your sibling and you two want to give your father/mother a birthday party. Discuss what preparations should be made for the party.

Text C

The Self-service

1 Read the following text aloud to your partner. Your partner listens to you without looking at the text.

If you are in a hurry and you want to have a quick meal, there is no better place than a self-service restaurant. You go into the restaurant, pick up a tray, knife, fork and spoon, and queue at a counter where the food is on display. You pick out what you want and put it on your tray which you have to push along a special rack till you reach the cashier. The cashier will give you the bill. After paying, you take your tray to any table you like. You can sit alone or with another customer. You can have a good meal in ten minutes. And as there is no waiter, you don't have to give a tip.

2 Your partner retells the story to you. Check if any information is missing in his/her retelling.

3 Search for information about the smart cafeteria in the Beijing 2022 Winter Olympics on the Internet and introduce it to your partner. And discuss with your partner what the future restaurant will look like and how people will be served.

Sentence-making

Pick out useful words and expressions from the following sentences and make sentences with them.

Example

Did you **have any trouble with** your Chinese when you were in Beijing?

▷ Mary is having some trouble with her computer.

- My mother made me dress up.
- I'd like to dance very much.
- There is no better place than a self-service restaurant.
- You don't have to give a tip.

Scripts

Text A   But the Chinese Did!¹

One day, Tom said to one of his friends, "I'm going to have a holiday in Beijing. But I don't speak Chinese, so I'll go to have Chinese lessons for a month before I go."

He studied very hard for a month, and then his holiday began and he went to China.

When he came back a few weeks later², his friend said to him, "Did you have any trouble with your Chinese³ when you were in Beijing, Tom?" "No, I didn't have any trouble with it," answered Tom. "But the Chinese did!"

Text B   At the Birthday Party

Mrs. Ross: Welcome, Peter. Give me your coat and hat.
Peter: Thank you, Mrs. Ross.
Mrs. Ross: The boys and girls are in the living room. Wait, I'll call John.

John: Hi, Peter. Why are you late?
Peter: My mother made me dress up⁴.
John: That's good. Alice has some pretty friends.

Peter: Happy birthday, Alice. Many happy returns of the day.⁵ Here's a present for you.
Alice: Thank you, Peter. Come into the dining room. I'm going to cut the cake soon.
John: Have some sandwiches, Peter.
Peter: Thanks. John, who's that girl?
John: That's Joan. She's pretty, isn't she? She likes to dance. Ask her to dance.
Peter: Well, I don't know.
John: Don't be afraid.
Peter: Who's afraid? I'm not afraid.

Peter: Would you like to dance, Joan?
Joan: Yes, thank you. I'd like to dance very much.

Notes

1　But the Chinese Did!: 但是中国人确实遇到了麻烦！

2　a few weeks later: 几个星期后

3　have any trouble with your Chinese: 讲中文时遇到任何麻烦

4　dress up: 打扮一下

5　Many happy returns of the day.: 祝年年有今朝，祝福用语。

Lesson 3

Text A

My Dishwasher

1 **Discuss briefly the questions with your partner.**

Does your mother or your father usually do housework? Who does the most housework? How do you think housework should be divided among family members?

2 **Listen to Text A once and answer the following questions.**

1   How many people are there in this story?

   _____

2   What is their relationship?

   _____

3   Had Mrs. Briggs lived in this street for a long time?

   _____

3 **Listen to Text A again. Take notes and answer the questions below.**

1   Where did Mrs. Williams live?

   _____

2   Who was her new neighbor?

   _____

3   What did the new neighbor like to talk about?

   _____

4   What did the new neighbor buy one day?

   _____

5   Why was the new neighbor extremely pleased with it?

   _____

6   How long did it take her to dry the dishes and plates?

   _____

7   Did Mrs. Williams have a dishwasher?

_____

8   What could Mrs. Williams' dishwasher do? How long had she had it?

_____

9   Was Mrs. Williams pleased with her dishwasher? Why?

_____

4 **Retell the story of Text A.**

1   Form a group of three or four and retell the story together. Take turns to give sentences until the story is completed. You may choose one of the following examples as the beginning of your story.

> • Mrs. Briggs moved into a new house in a small street in London. She spent several weeks furnishing her new house.
> • Mrs. Briggs was my new neighbor. She was very talkative and liked to show off.
> • One day, I bought a new dishwasher. I liked it very much.

2   Regroup with students from different groups in step 1. Each student retells the story from his/her previous group.

5 **Discuss the following questions in groups of three or four. After the discussion, select one member of your group to report to the class what you have talked about.**

1   Use as many descriptive words as you can to describe Mrs. Williams and Mrs. Briggs.

2   Would Mrs. Williams and Mrs. Briggs be good friends? Why/Why not?

Text B

Summer Plans

1 **Listen to Text B once and answer the following questions.**

1   How many people are involved in the dialogue?

_____

2   What are they talking about?

_____

3   Has Mary been camping before?

_____

2 **Listen to Text B again. Take notes and answer the questions below.**

1   Who are the people in the dialogue? What is the possible relationship between them?

_____

2   What time of the year is it?

_____

3   What is Mary going to do in the summer vacation?

_____

4   What is Peter going to do this summer?

_____

5   What is John going to do this summer?

_____

6   Will Peter be able to see John before going camping?

_____

7   When will they meet again?

_____

3 **Describe to your partner the picture below with the following words and expressions.**

a blond-haired boy
about fifteen years old
wear a striped sweater
a pair of dark-colored trousers
lean against a branch of a tree
hands resting on the branch of the tree
look at the girl
talk to
tall and slim
in a pullover and a short skirt
a flower in the right hand
hold it to her nose
a hand on the tree trunk
an old tree

4 Suppose you are Mary and your partner plays the role of Peter. You two are talking about what you usually do for the summer/winter vacation. Describe to your partner an outing experience that you can never forget.

Text C

Who Waits for Whom?

1 Read the following text aloud to your partner. Your partner listens to you without looking at the text.

Mr. and Mrs. Allen go grocery shopping on Saturday mornings. Mr. Allen never enjoys these trips. Mrs. Allen does the shopping and he sits in the car and waits for her.

This morning, there were a lot of people and it took Mrs. Allen longer than usual. An hour went by and finally a man came up to Mr. Allen. "Excuse me," he said, "is your name Allen? Your wife is waiting for you at the checkout counter. Her cellphone is powered off and she can't pay for the groceries!"

2 Your partner retells the story to you. Check if any information is missing in his/her retelling.

3 Tell your partner why you think Mr. Allen did not enjoy going shopping.

Sentence-making

Pick out useful words and expressions from the following sentences and make sentences with them.

Example

That **sounds wonderful**!

➢ What he talked about sounds wonderful.

- She talked a lot about her expensive furniture.
- I've had a dishwasher for twelve and a half years.
- I have been camping four times.
- Mr. and Mrs. Allen go grocery shopping on Saturday mornings.
- An hour went by.

Scripts

Text A   My Dishwasher

Mrs. Williams lived in a small street in London, and now she had a new neighbor[1]. Her name was Mrs. Briggs, and she talked a lot about[2] her expensive furniture, her beautiful carpets and her new kitchen[3]. "Do you know," she said to Mrs. Williams one day, "I've got a new dishwasher[4]. It washes the plates and glasses and knives and forks beautifully[5]." "Oh?" Mrs. Williams answered. "And does it dry[6] them and put them in the cupboard[7] too?" Mrs. Briggs was surprised.

"Well," she answered, "the things[8] in the machine[9] are dry after an hour, but it doesn't put them away[10], of course." "I've had a dishwasher for twelve and a half years," Mrs. Williams said. "Oh?" Mrs. Briggs answered. "And does yours put the things in the cupboard when it has washed them?" She laughed nastily.[11] "Yes, he does," Mrs. Williams answered. "He dries the dishes and puts them away."

Text B　Summer Plans

Peter and Mary are talking about their plans for the summer[12]. Mary is going to work in the city, but Peter is going to camp[13]. Mary thinks that their friend John is going to the mountains with his family.

Peter:　What are you going to do after you return from Washington[14]?

Mary:　I'm going to stay in the city[15].

Peter:　What will you do all day[16]?

Mary:　I'm going to work with my father at the store[17]. In the evening, I'll read books. On weekends[18], I'll go to the beach[19] with my family.

Peter:　Have you ever worked?

Mary:　No, but I can learn. What are you going to do this summer?

Peter:　I'm going to camp. I have been camping four times.

Mary:　I have never been camping. What will you do there?

Peter:　We do many things. In the morning, we go swimming and boating[20]. In the afternoon, we play basketball or tennis. We sit around a campfire[21] at night[22]. We sing or tell stories.

Mary:　That sounds wonderful.[23]

Peter:　It is wonderful.[24] What's John going to do this summer?

Mary:　I think he's going to the mountains with his parents.

Peter:　Well, so long[25], Mary. Have fun.[26]

Mary:　You too[27], Peter. Give my regards to John.[28] I'll see you in September.

Notes

1　a new neighbor: 一个新邻居

2　talked a lot about: 对……谈论很多

3　her expensive furniture, her beautiful carpets and her new kitchen: 她的名贵家具、漂亮的地毯和崭新的厨房

4　a new dishwasher: 一台新的洗碗机

5　beautifully:（洗得）非常好

6　dry: 弄干

7　the cupboard: 碗橱

8   the things: 指的是碗、叉、勺等餐具

9   in the machine: 在洗碗机里

10   put them away: 把它们收起来

11   She laughed nastily.: 她不怀好意地大笑起来。

12   are talking about their plans for the summer: 正在谈论他们的暑期计划

13   camp: 宿营

14   after you return from Washington: 你从华盛顿回来之后

15   stay in the city: 待在城里

16   all day: 整天

17   work with my father at the store: 在商店里同我爸爸一起干活

18   On weekends: 在周末

19   go to the beach: 去海滩

20   go swimming and boating: 去游泳和划船

21   sit around a campfire: 围坐在篝火边

22   at night: 在夜里

23   That sounds wonderful.: 听起来真美妙。

24   It is wonderful.: 这的确很美妙。

25   so long: 再见

26   Have fun.: 玩得开心。

27   You too: 祝你也玩得开心

28   Give my regards to John.: 代我向约翰问好。

Lesson 4

Text A

After a Heavy Snowstorm

1 **Discuss briefly the questions with your partner.**

Have you ever been caught in a snowstorm? Or have you ever seen a snowstorm in a film or on TV? Describe what you saw.

2 **Listen to Text A once and answer the following questions.**

1 How many people are there in the story?

_____

2 Who are they?

_____

3 What is the relationship between them?

_____

3 **Listen to Text A again. Take notes and answer the questions below.**

1 What happened one night?

_____

2 What was Mr. Smith's garden like in the morning?

_____

3 What did Mr. Smith want to do?

_____

4 Did Mr. Smith clean the snow himself?

_____

5 Who cleaned the snow for Mr. Smith?

_____

6 Could the man throw any snow on the bushes? Why not?

_____

7   Did Mr. Smith stay at home while the man was cleaning the snow?

_____

8   What did Mr. Smith do?

_____

9   What was the garden like when Mr. Smith came back?

_____

10   How did Mr. Smith feel?

_____

11   What did Mr. Smith find when he opened the garage?

_____

12   Could Mr. Smith get his car out? Why not?

_____

4   Retell the story of Text A.

1   Form a group of three or four and retell the story together. Take turns to give sentences until the story is completed. You may choose one of the following examples as the beginning of your story.

- Mr. Smith drove to work every morning. One day he couldn't get his car out of the garage.
- Mr. Smith had never been late for work. But one night there was a heavy snowstorm and the next morning he arrived at his office half an hour late.
- One morning there was deep snow everywhere. Someone called me and asked me to clean the snow in his garden.

2   Regroup with students from different groups in step 1. Each student retells the story from his/her previous group.

5   Discuss the following questions in groups of three or four. After the discussion, select one member of your group to report to the class what you have talked about.

1   What would you say to the man when you asked him to clean the snow in your garden if you were Mr. Smith?

2   Who was to blame for the snow in the garage, Mr. Smith or the man who was paid to clean the snow? Why?

3   What would you say to the man after seeing the snow in the garage if you were Mr. Smith? What would you do next?

Text B

No Baseball Today.

1 **Listen to Text B once and answer the following questions.**

1 Who are the two people in this dialogue?

_____

2 What are they talking about?

_____

3 Where are they in the first part of the dialogue?

_____

4 Where are they in the second part of the dialogue?

_____

2 **Listen to Text B again. Take notes and answer the questions below.**

1 Who wants to play baseball today?

_____

2 Why can't John join him?

_____

3 Who are going to move tomorrow?

_____

4 Where is the new house?

_____

5 What does Peter offer to do?

_____

6 What does Peter do first?

_____

7 What does John ask Peter to do after he has finished it?

_____

8 Does Peter finish the work quickly? Why not?

_____

9 What does Peter want to borrow? Why?

_____

3 **Describe to your partner the picture below with the following words and expressions.**

a dark-haired boy
tall and athletic
be dressed in a black sweater
wear a tie
hold a thick book in his hands
put it into the box in front of...
smile at
feel pleased with
a blond-haired boy
not as tall as the other one
wear a light-colored sweater and a dark-colored shirt
hold a book in his right hand
show the book to the other one
look at the cover of the book in his left hand
be interested in the book
a small paper box in front of them
with some books in it
some books lying around the box to be packed

4 Suppose you are John and your partner plays the role of Peter. What would you say when Peter reads the magazines instead of packing them?

Text C

An Accident

1 Read the following text aloud to your partner. Your partner listens to you without looking at the text.

> The river, you see, was never really safe at that time of the year—early autumn, I mean, when there is heavy rainfall. So when I heard the children had gone swimming, as they usually did all spring and summer, I knew there might be an awful accident. And when they came home late without little Katie, I guessed what had happened.

2 Your partner retells the story to you. Check if any information is missing in his/her retelling.

3 Ask your partner what he/she thinks had happened to Katie and why he/she thinks so. You can also share your answers with your partner.

Sentence-making

Pick out useful words and expressions from the following sentences and make sentences with them.

Example

In the morning Mr. Smith's garden **was full of** deep snow.

> ➢ I woke up in the middle of the night and found the room was full of smoke.
> ➢ The textbook is full of new words.

- One night there was a heavy snowstorm.
- …so he paid a man to clean the path from his garage to his gate.
- Don't throw any snow on the street, or the police will be angry.
- Mr. Smith was very pleased until he opened the garage to get his car out.
- And his car was somewhere under it all!
- I have to help my mother.
- Is it far from here?
- Can I help you pack?
- The river, you see, was never really safe at that time of the year.
- …as they usually did all spring and summer, I knew there might be an awful accident.

Scripts

Text A   After a Heavy Snowstorm[1]

One night there was a heavy snowstorm, and in the morning Mr. Smith's garden was full of deep snow[2]. Mr. Smith wanted to take his car out[3], so he paid a man to clean the path[4] from his garage to his gate[5]. He said to this man, "Don't throw any snow on that side, because it will damage the bushes[6] in my garden; and don't throw any snow on the street, or[7] the police will be angry." Then Mr. Smith went out.

When he came back, the path was clean and the snow from it was not on the bushes, or the fence[8], or the street. Mr. Smith was very pleased[9] until he opened the garage to get his car out! The garage was full to the top with all the snow[10] from the path, and his car was somewhere under it all[11]!

Text B   No Baseball Today.

Peter: Can you play baseball with me[12] today?

John: No, I can't. I'm sorry. I have to help my mother. We're going to move[13] tomorrow.

Peter: Where's the new house? Is it far from here?[14]

John: No, it's not far. It's near our old house.

Peter: Can I help you pack?[15]

John: Sure.[16] Thanks.

Peter: What can I do?

John: Take the books out of the bookcase[17]. Put them in the box.

An hour later.

Peter: Well, the books are in the box. What can I do now?

John: Take the magazines out of the bookcase. Put them in that box.

Peter: All right.

John: Peter! Pack them. Don't read them.[18]

Peter: These magazines are interesting. May I borrow one?

John: Of course.

Peter: Thanks, John.

Notes

1　a Heavy Snowstorm: 一场很大的暴风雪

2　was full of deep snow: 到处是厚厚的积雪

3　take his car out: 把他的车开出来

4　he paid a man to clean the path: 他花钱雇人来清扫小道

5　from his garage to his gate: 从车库到大门

6　the bushes: 灌木丛

7　or: 否则

8　the fence: 栅栏

9　was very pleased: 非常满意

10　was full to the top with all the snow: 满满的都是雪，直到房顶

11　his car was somewhere under it all: 他的车埋在雪下的某处

12　play baseball with me: 同我打棒球

13　move: 搬家

14　Is it far from here?: 离这儿远吗？

15　Can I help you pack?: 我帮你打包好吗？

16　Sure.: 当然。

17　the bookcase: 书柜

18　Peter! Pack them. Don't read them.: 彼得，把杂志打包，装起来，别看了。

Lesson 5

Text A

Stop Eating Fried Potatoes.

1 **Discuss briefly the questions with your partner.**

What kinds of food do you think are bad for health? Name some and explain why.

2 **Listen to Text A once and answer the following questions.**

1 What is the story about?

_____

2 Where did the conversation take place?

_____

3 What should Mrs. Jenkins stop doing?

_____

3 **Listen to Text A again. Take notes and answer the questions below.**

1 What did Mrs. Jenkins do one day?

_____

2 Why did she go there?

_____

3 How did the doctor treat her?

_____

4 What did the doctor say Mrs. Jenkins should do to get well again?

_____

5 Did Mrs. Jenkins smoke?

_____

6 What else did the doctor ask Mrs. Jenkins not to do when she said that she didn't drink alcohol?

_____

7   What did Mrs. Jenkins drink every day?

_____

8   Did the doctor eventually mention anything that Mrs. Jenkins liked?

_____

9   Do you think it was necessary for Mrs. Jenkins to give up what she liked eating?

_____

4   **Retell the story of Text A.**

1   Form a group of three or four and retell the story together. Take turns to give sentences until the story is completed. You may choose one of the following examples as the beginning of your story.

- Mrs. Jenkins was not in good health. She had some trouble with her heart.
- I was worried about my health. So I went to see my doctor.
- One of my patients had a heart condition. I gave her some advice.

2   Regroup with students from different groups in step 1. Each student retells the story from his/her previous group.

5   **Discuss the following questions in groups of three or four. After the discussion, select one member of your group to report to the class what you have talked about.**

1   Describe the doctor by using as many descriptive words as you can.
2   Do you think the doctor had given Mrs. Jenkins good advice? Why?
3   Would you stop eating fried potatoes if you were Mrs. Jenkins? Why?

Text B

Keep Him in Bed.

1 **Listen to Text B once and answer the following questions.**

1 What is the story about?

_____

2 How do the people in the conversation relate to each other?

_____

3 Who did Mrs. Welsh talk to?

_____

2 **Listen to Text B again. Take notes and answer the questions below.**

1 Why do you think Mrs. Welsh asked Peter to get up?

_____

2 Did Peter get up immediately?

_____

3 Why didn't he get up?

_____

4 What was wrong with him according to Peter?

_____

5 What did Mrs. Welsh say Peter was suffering from?

_____

6 What was Mrs. Welsh going to do?

_____

7 What was the doctor's name?

_____

8 What did Mrs. Welsh ask him to do?

_____

9 What questions did Dr. Dawes ask Mrs. Welsh?

_____

10 What did the doctor ask her to do?

_____

11 What is the address of the Welsh's?

_____

12 Would the doctor go to see the patient?

_____

3 **Describe to your partner the picture below with the following words and expressions.**

in a bedroom
a thick blanket
a soft pillow
a single bed
a bedside lamp
a bedside table
a boy in his teens
lie on his back
lie in bed ill
lie in bed in pajamas
lie in bed covered with a thick blanket
lie in bed motionless
lie in bed with one's eyes closed
look ill
look pale
have a fever
look red on one's cheeks
feel sick
feel cold
not feel like eating
lose one's appetite

have a sore throat/headache
look young for one's age
don't look like a person who has a teenage son
curly hair
be dressed in dark
look worried
call a doctor
have an ambulance sent
speak in a trembling voice
ask for sick leave
appear nervous
be at a loss what to do
be scared

4 **Suppose you are not feeling well. Talk with your partner about the symptoms you have and whether you should go to see a doctor or not.**

Text C

The Man with a Black Bag

1 **Play the audio of the following text to your partner. Your partner listens without looking at the text.**

Harry is looking at a man in the street. He is talking to Jack about the man.

Harry: Who's that man with the black bag?
Jack: I can't see a man with a black bag.
Harry: He was standing at the door of that house a moment ago. Now he's walking down the street.
Jack: Oh, that man. I don't know who he is. He's a stranger.
Harry: Look at the man who's running after him.
Jack: Yes. Perhaps the stranger is a thief.

> Harry: I don't think so.
> Jack: Wait a minute. I can recognize the man who's running after him. It's Mr. Green.
> Harry: Now I remember. Mr. Green told me yesterday that his brother was coming.

2 **Your partner retells what the conversation is about. Check if any information is missing in his/her retelling.**

3 **Ask your partner what he/she would do if he/she sees a thief in the street. You can also share with your partner what you would do if you see a thief in the street.**

Sentence-making

Pick out useful words and expressions from the following sentences and make sentences with them.

Example

Mrs. Jenkins **went to** her doctor one day.

> ▷ Mary went to her mother that morning.
> ▷ We are going to our parents for the weekend.
> ▷ Tom has gone to his tutor.

- Her heart was giving her trouble.
- Stop smoking.
- I don't like smoking.
- The doctor thought for a few seconds.
- He got up to say goodbye to Mrs. Jenkins.
- Keep him in bed.
- What's the matter with you?
- I can't get out of bed.
- Look at the man who's running after him.
- Perhaps the stranger is a thief.

Scripts

Text A   Stop Eating Fried Potatoes.

Mrs. Jenkins went to her doctor one day, because her heart was giving her trouble[1]. The doctor listened to her heart carefully and did a few other checks. Then he said, "Well, Mrs. Jenkins, stop smoking[2], and then you'll soon be quite all right[3] again."

"But doctor," answered Mrs. Jenkins quickly, "I've never smoked. I don't like smoking."

"Oh, well," said the doctor, "then don't drink any more alcohol[4]."

"But I don't drink alcohol," answered Mrs. Jenkins at once[5].

"Stop drinking tea and coffee then," the doctor said to her.

"I only drink water," answered Mrs. Jenkins, "I don't like tea or coffee."

The doctor thought for a few seconds[6] and then said, "Well...er...do you like fried potatoes[7]?"

"Yes, I like them very much," answered Mrs. Jenkins.

"All right, then stop eating those," said the doctor as he got up to say goodbye[8] to Mrs. Jenkins.

Text B   Keep Him in Bed.[9]

Mrs. Welsh:	Get up[10], Peter. It's late.
Peter:	I can't get up, Mom. I'm ill.
Mrs. Welsh:	What's the matter with you?[11]
Peter:	I have a headache and a bad stomachache[12].
Mrs. Welsh:	You have a fever too. I'm going to call Dr. Dawes. Don't get out of bed.
Peter:	Oh, I can't get out of bed. I'm too ill.
Mrs. Welsh:	Hello, this is Mrs. Welsh. Is Dr. Dawes there? Thank you. I'll wait...Dr. Dawes, this is Mrs. Welsh. Can you come to the house, please?
Dr. Dawes:	Who's ill?
Mrs. Welsh:	Peter, my son.
Dr. Dawes:	What's the matter with him?
Mrs. Welsh:	I don't know. He has a headache, a bad stomachache and a fever.
Dr. Dawes:	Keep him in bed. Where do you live?
Mrs. Welsh:	We live at 44 Washington Avenue[13].
Dr. Dawes:	All right, Mrs. Welsh, I'll be there soon.
Mrs. Welsh:	Thank you. Goodbye, Dr. Dawes.

Notes

1　her heart was giving her trouble: 她的心脏使她难受

2　stop smoking: 戒烟

3　you'll soon be quite all right: 你很快会好的

4　don't drink any more alcohol: 不要再喝酒了

5　at once: 马上

6　thought for a few seconds: 想了几秒钟

7　do you like fried potatoes: 你喜欢炸土豆吗

8　got up to say goodbye: 站起来说再见

9　Keep Him in Bed.: 让他卧床。

10　Get up: 起床

11　What's the matter with you?: 你怎么啦?

12　a bad stomachache: 肚子很痛

13　44 Washington Avenue: 华盛顿大街 44 号

Lesson 6

Text A

A Beautiful Dress

1 **Discuss briefly the questions with your partner.**

Do you often shop? Describe an experience of doing shopping with your parents or with your friends.

2 **Listen to Text A once and answer the following questions.**

1 What is the story about?

_____

2 How many people are there in the story?

_____

3 What is their relationship?

_____

3 **Listen to Text A again. Take notes and answer the questions below.**

1 Where did Mrs. Jones go one day?

_____

2 What did she see in the window of a shop?

_____

3 Did she like it? How do you know?

_____

4 Did her husband give her the money to buy it right away? Why not?

_____

5 Did Mrs. Jones give up the idea of buying the dress?

_____

6 What did she do then?

_____

7   Did Mrs. Jones get the money to buy the dress in the end?

_____

8   Was her husband interested in the dress? How do you know?

_____

9   Did Mrs. Jones buy the dress after her husband gave her the money? Why?

_____

10   Do you think Mrs. Jones was a smart buyer? Why?

_____

4 Retell the story of Text A.

1   Form a group of three or four and retell the story together. Take turns to give sentences until the story is completed. You may choose one of the following examples as the beginning of your story.

> - Mrs. Jones loved pretty dresses very much. She often tried to get money from her husband to buy them.
> - In the window of a shop, there was a pretty cotton dress on display. It cost 120 pounds, which was pretty expensive.
> - Mr. Jones came home from work one day. He found that his wife was very happy.

2   Regroup with students from different groups in step 1. Each student retells the story from his/her previous group.

5 Discuss the following questions in groups of three or four. After the discussion, select one member of your group to report to the class what you have talked about.

1   Use as many descriptive words as you can to describe Mr. and Mrs. Jones.
2   Do you think Mr. Jones knew his wife's shopping habit well? Explain.
3   Explain to your group mates about your shopping habits.

Text B

Which Bus Shall I Take?

1 **Listen to Text B once and answer the following questions.**

1 What is the dialogue about?

_____

2 What are the names of the two speakers?

_____

3 Where do they meet?

_____

2 **Listen to Text B again. Take notes and answer the questions below.**

1 Where is Jane going?

_____

2 Who is Susan Green? And where is she?

_____

3 Does Jane know how to get to the hospital?

_____

4 How do you think Henry got to know the way to the hospital?

_____

5 Did Henry have to wait for a No. 7 bus when he went to visit Susan?

_____

6 Which bus did Henry take?

_____

7 Which bus runs more frequently, Bus No. 7 or Bus No. 13?

_____

8 Which of the two is more convenient?

_____

9 Which one do you think Jane will take?

_____

3 Describe to your partner the picture below with the following words and expressions.

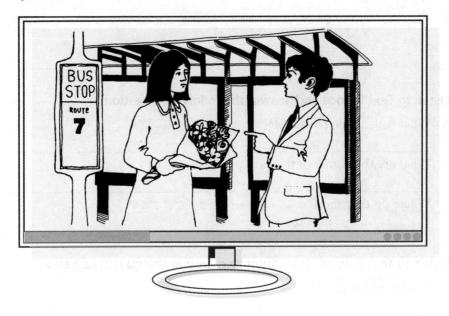

a young woman
straight hair
be plainly dressed
hold a bunch of flowers
a gift for a sick friend
stand at a bus stop
a busy street
a young man in a suit
point to the flowers
seem to be asking questions
talk about their mutual friend
be concerned about the patient
a kind and gentle man

4 Suppose you are Jane and your partner is Susan Green, who is hospitalized. What would you say when you visit her?

Text C

Volunteer in the Fight Against Desertification.

1 **Read the following text aloud to your partner. Your partner listens to you without looking at the text.**

> Liu Zhizhuo, 23, is the founder of an environmental organization and a volunteer in the fight against desertification. He was honored as one of "The Most Beautiful Chinese College Students" of 2020 by the Ministry of Education. Since 2016, Liu has been growing plants in Minqin County, which is surrounded by the Badain Jaran and Tengger Deserts in Gansu Province.
>
> During the summer of 2016, Liu and eight of his peers arrived in Minqin. They would soon develop a routine, waking up at 6 a.m. and heading toward the Tengger Desert with grass squares, seeds of trees, and the necessary tools. They would usually stay in the desert for several days. Their skin would burn under strong, ultraviolet rays, and sand blown by wind gusts would sting their eyes. But during their first night in the desert, they enjoyed stargazing. "Watching the stars that night will be a special memory for us," Liu said.

2 **Your partner retells the story to you. Check if any information is missing in his/her retelling.**

3 **Ask your partner what he/she can learn from Liu Zhizhuo and what he/she can do to make university life more meaningful. You can also share your opinion with your partner.**

Sentence-making

Pick out useful words and expressions from the following sentences and make sentences with them.

Example

Mr. Jones **came back from** work.

➤ Tom comes back from school at four every afternoon.
➤ Liu will come back from hospital when she is better.

- One day, Mrs. Jones went shopping.
- She began to tell him about a beautiful cotton dress.
- Here is the money!
- Jane is on her way to the hospital to see her friend.
- Must I catch a No. 7 bus to get there?
- A No. 13 bus will take you there.
- I had to wait for half an hour at the bus stop.
- He was honored as one of "The Most Beautiful Chinese College Students" of 2020.
- Since 2016, Liu has been growing plants in Minqin County.
- During the summer of 2016, Liu and eight of his peers arrived in Minqin.

Scripts

Text A   A Beautiful Dress

One day, Mrs. Jones went shopping[1]. When her husband came back from work[2] in the evening, she began to tell him about a beautiful cotton dress[3]. "I saw it in a shop this morning," she said, "and..."

"And you want to buy it," said her husband. "How much does it cost?"

"One hundred and twenty pounds.[4]"

"One hundred and twenty pounds for a cotton dress? That is too much!"

But every evening afterward, when Mr. Jones came back from work, his wife continued to speak only about the dress[5], and at last[6], after a week, he said, "Oh, buy the dress! Here is the money![7]" She was very happy.

But the next evening, when Mr. Jones came home and asked, "Have you got the famous dress?" she said, "No."

"Why not?" he said.

"Well, it was still in the window of the shop[8] after a week, so I thought, nobody else wants this dress, so I don't want it either."

Text B   Which Bus Shall I Take?

Jane Foster has just met Henry Taylor. Jane is on her way to[9] the hospital to see her friend, Susan Green.

Henry: Where are you going, Jane?

Jane: I'm going to the hospital to see Susan Green.

Henry: I saw her yesterday. She was a little better[10].

Jane: Must I catch a No. 7 bus[11] to get there?

Henry: No, you needn't. A No. 13 bus will also take you to the hospital.

Jane: No. 13 buses run much more frequently[12], don't they?

Henry: Yes. I took a No. 7 bus yesterday, and I waited for half an hour at the bus stop.

Jane: Thank you, Henry. I'll get a No. 13[13].

Henry: But No. 13 buses leave from the center of the town. You'll have to walk[14] two miles to catch one.

Notes

1   went shopping: 去买东西
2   came back from work: 下班回来
3   tell him about a beautiful cotton dress: 告诉他有关一件漂亮的棉布连衣裙
4   One hundred and twenty pounds.: 120 英镑。
5   continued to speak only about the dress: 继续只谈裙子的事
6   at last: 终于
7   Here is the money!: 给你钱！
8   in the window of the shop: 在商店的橱窗里
9   on her way to: 在她去……的路上
10 a little better: （比原来）好了一些

11   catch a No. 7 bus: 乘 7 路汽车

12   run much more frequently: （汽车）来的次数要多得多

13   get a No. 13: 乘 13 路汽车

14   You'll have to walk: 你得步行

Lesson 7

Text A

A Visit to Conwy Castle

1 **Discuss briefly the questions with your partner.**

Have you ever visited some places of interest? Describe one of the visits to your partner.

2 **Listen to Text A once and answer the following questions.**

1 What is the story about?

_____

2 Who are the people in the story?

_____

3 What subject are the students learning?

_____

3 **Listen to Text A again. Take notes and answer the questions below.**

1 What did the teacher tell the students one day?

_____

2 How and when were they going there?

_____

3 What did they go to see there?

_____

4 Why were they going to Conwy?

_____

5 How old was the castle?

_____

6 When did the boys arrive at school on Friday?

_____

7　What did they do then?

_____

8　What did Dave's mother want to know when he got home after the visit?

_____

9　What didn't Dave like about the castle?

_____

4　**Retell the story of Text A.**

1　Form a group of three or four and retell the story together. Take turns to give sentences until the story is completed. You may choose one of the following examples as the beginning of your story.

> - I was a teacher of English history. I decided to take the boys to visit a beautiful castle.
> - One day, my son came back from school. He told me their history teacher would take them to a beautiful castle.
> - English history was one of my favorite subjects in school because we were often taken to visit some places of interest.

2　Regroup with students from different groups in step 1. Each student retells the story from his/her previous group.

5　**Discuss the following questions in groups of three or four. After the discussion, select one member of your group to report to the class what you have talked about.**

1　Do you think visiting historical sites is a good way of learning history? Why?
2　Do you think the Conwy Castle was built too close to the railway?
3　How would you answer Dave's question about the railway?

Text B

New Year's Resolutions

1　**Listen to Text B once and answer the following questions.**

1　How many people are there in the conversation?

_____

2   Who are they?

_____

3   What are they talking about?

_____

2 **Listen to Text B again. Take notes and answer the questions below.**

1   What does John ask Peter?

_____

2   What does Peter tell him?

_____

3   When and where did Peter buy the Christmas decorations?

_____

4   What does Peter invite John to do?

_____

5   Why can't John go with him?

_____

6   Who joins the boys in talking?

_____

7   What does Mary ask the boys?

_____

8   What do they say in reply?

_____

9   Is Mary going to make any New Year's resolutions this year?

_____

10   Does she want to tell the boys about her New Year's resolutions?

_____

3 **Describe to your partner the picture below with the following words and expressions.**

semi-detached houses

the Northern hemisphere

two-storey houses

a front porch

in front of

welcome another white Christmas

snow covering everything, the houses, the trees and the streets

two schoolboys

a boy with light/dark hair

on their way from

in a jacket

in a winter overcoat

talk about something pleasant

look happy

look forward to

a big occasion

a family reunion

4 **Tell your partner what people usually do in your family/town/city to celebrate the New Year and what you wish to accomplish in the coming year.**

Text C

A Busy Afternoon

1 **Play the audio of the following text to your partner. Your partner listens without looking at the text.**

> Frank is very busy. He is talking to Jimmy, his best friend.
>
> Jimmy: Did you play football yesterday?
> Frank: Yes, I played with Tony and John.
> Jimmy: What did you do after you'd played football?
> Frank: We all went swimming.
> Jimmy: Are you going swimming again this afternoon?
> Frank: No, we aren't. We're going to help Mr. Smith to plant some flowers.
> Jimmy: Are you helping him all afternoon?
> Frank: Yes, we are. We can neither play football nor do our homework today.
> Jimmy: You're going to be very busy.
> Frank: Yes, we certainly are. But Mr. Smith is going to pay us for all the work we'll do.

2 **Your partner retells what the conversation is about. Check if any information is missing in his/her retelling.**

3 **Ask your partner about one of his/her busy days. You can also share with your partner what you did on one of your busy days.**

Sentence-making

Pick out useful words and expressions from the following sentences and make sentences with them.

Example

On Friday, the boys came to school at 9 o'clock and **got on** the bus.

➢ As soon as he got on the car, it started moving.

- There's a beautiful castle there, and we're going to visit it.
- The boys were very happy when they heard this.
- Did you like the castle, Dave?
- Peter invites John to see the Christmas tree at his house.
- I make them, but I break them the next day.
- What did you do after you'd played football?
- Are you helping him all afternoon?
- But Mr. Smith is going to pay us for all the work we'll do.

Scripts

Text A   A Visit to Conwy Castle[1]

Dave's class at school were studying English history, and one day, their teacher said to them, "Well, boys, on Friday we're all going to get on a bus and go to Conwy[2]. There's a beautiful castle there, and we're going to visit it." The boys were very happy when they heard this[3].

"Now, has anybody got any questions[4]?" the teacher asked.

"How old is the castle, sir?" Dave asked.

"It's about eight hundred years old, Dave," the teacher answered.

"What's the name of the castle, sir?" another boy asked.

"Conwy Castle," the teacher said.

On Friday, the boys came to school at 9 o'clock and got on the bus. They visited

Conwy Castle, and then they came back and went home[5].

"Well," Dave's mother said to him when he got home, "did you like the castle, Dave?"

"Not very much," Dave answered. "The people built it too near the railway.[6]"

Text B　New Year's Resolutions[7]

Peter and John are admiring the Christmas decorations[8] on the houses. Peter invites John to see the Christmas tree at his house, but John can't go. He has to buy a present for his mother. Later the boys and Mary talk about New Year's resolutions.

Peter:　I'm glad we live in a small town.

John:　Why?

Peter:　Because the houses look so nice at Christmas time.

John:　Yes, they do. Do you have a Christmas tree this year?

Peter:　Yes, we have a big tree this year. I bought the decorations at the one-pound shop[9] yesterday. Do you want to come and see it?

John:　I can't now because I have to buy a present for my mother.

Peter:　When can you come?

John:　I don't know when I can come. I'll let you know later.

Mary:　Hi, boys. Are you going to make any New Year's resolutions this year?

Peter:　No, I never make any.

John:　I make them, but I break them the next day. Are you making any, Mary?

Mary:　Yes, but I can't tell you what they are.

Notes

1　Conwy Castle: 康威城堡，位于威尔士，是中世纪用于防御的城堡

2　get on a bus and go to Conwy: 坐公共汽车去康威

3　when they heard this: 当他们听到这个消息时

4　has anybody got any questions: 还有谁有什么问题吗

5　then they came back and went home: 然后他们又回到学校，之后才回家

6　The people built it too near the railway.: 人们把城堡建得离铁路太近了。

7　New Year's Resolutions: 新年时下的决心

8　are admiring the Christmas decorations: 正在欣赏圣诞节装饰品

9　the one-pound shop: 出售廉价小商品的杂货店，商品的价格通常为一英镑，故有此名

Lesson 8

Text A

A Tall and Slim Girl

1 **Discuss briefly the questions with your partner.**

Have you ever been unsure of yourself? How did you feel? How did you deal with it? Share your experience with your partner.

2 **Listen to Text A once and answer the following questions.**

1   Who is the story about?

2   Can you roughly guess her age?

3   Was she a proud girl? Why do you think so?

3 **Listen to Text A again. Take notes and answer the questions below.**

1   How tall was Rosa?

2   What grade was she in? Who was the tallest in her grade?

3   What did she worry about?

4   What was her mother's advice to her?

5   How did Rosa feel after she heard her mother's words?

6   Who was Mr. Ransom?

7   What did he ask Rosa to do? Why?

_____

8   Did Rosa feel better? Why?

_____

4   Retell the story of Text A.

1   Form a group of three or four and retell the story together. Take turns to give sentences until the story is completed. You may choose one of the following examples as the beginning of your story.

> • Rosa was a beautiful girl. She was tall and slim.
> • Rosa's mother was worried about her. Though she was tall and slim, Rosa didn't want to stand up straight.
> • When I was in the sixth grade, I was five feet six inches tall. In fact, I was the tallest in my grade. I wasn't happy about my height.

2   Regroup with students from different groups in step 1. Each student retells the story from his/her previous group.

5   Discuss the following questions in groups of three or four. After the discussion, select one member of your group to report to the class what you have talked about.

1   Why do you think children don't want to be different from others?
2   What do you think parents and teachers should do to help a child to be confident?

Text B

What a Mess!

1   Listen to Text B once and answer the following questions.

1   How many people are talking in this dialogue?

_____

2   Where are they?

_____

3   What are they talking about?

_____

2 Listen to Text B again. Take notes and answer the questions below.

1   What has Bill done? Does he do it on purpose?

_____

2   What does Mr. Field say about it?

_____

3   Who was more careless than Bill? What did he do?

_____

4   Who else were to blame for what John had done?

_____

5   What did the headmaster ask the workmen to do?

_____

6   Why isn't there a notice?

_____

7   Are the workmen back?

_____

8   What are they doing?

_____

9   Who is the most careless of all? Why?

_____

3 Describe to your partner the picture below with the following words and expressions.

a teenager

look like a high school student

stand in the garden

wear a jacket with a chest pocket

a dark-haired boy

hold his right hand up

be stained with paint

annoyed

don't know what to do

a cement path leading to the gate of the garden

several footprints on the path

walk across the wet cement

a bucket near the gate

a bag of cement beside the bucket

a board on the grass with some cement on it

a shovel placed on the board against the cement bag

wooden fences around the garden

some trees outside the garden

4 **Suppose you are Bill and your partner plays the role of Mr. Field. What would you say when Mr. Field talks to you about the mess? Make a conversation.**

Text C

Better Be a Stupid Man.

1 **Read the following text aloud to your partner. Your partner listens to you without looking at the text.**

It was a beautiful spring morning. There wasn't a cloud in the sky, and the sun was warm but not too hot, so Mr. Andrews was surprised when he saw an old gentleman at the bus stop with a big, strong black umbrella in his hand.

Mr. Andrews said to him, "Are we going to have rain today, do you think?"

"No," said the old gentleman, "I don't think so."

"Then are you carrying the umbrella to keep the sun off you?"

"No, the sun is not very hot in spring."

Mr. Andrews looked at the big umbrella again, and the gentleman said, "I am an old man, and my legs are not very strong, so I really need a walking stick. But when I carry a walking stick, people say, 'Look at that poor old man,' and I don't like that. When I carry an umbrella in fine weather, people only say, 'Look at that stupid man.'"

2 Your partner retells the story to you. Check if any information is missing in his/her retelling.

3 Ask your partner if he/she thinks it is better to be stupid than to be old and why he/she thinks so. You can also share your answers with your partner. You can start with your agreement or disagreement with your partner's opinion.

Sentence-making

Pick out useful words and expressions from the following sentences and make sentences with them.

Example

You **mustn't** touch the wet paint, Bill.

➢ You mustn't speak to your uncle rudely.

➢ You mustn't walk across the wet cement.

➢ You mustn't watch TV late into the night.

- At five feet six inches, Rosa was taller than every other student in the sixth grade.
- She worried about this all the time, in school and at home.
- But she was still afraid her classmates were making fun of her behind her back.

- He said that Rosa was a good basketball player and her height would make her valuable as the center.
- Try to be more careful in future.
- I wasn't as careless as John Sampson.
- He walked across that wet cement over there.
- The workmen oughtn't to leave it without a notice.
- Here they come with it now!
- They've forgotten about the wet cement and they're walking across it to put up the notice!
- Mr. Andrews was surprised when he saw an old gentleman at the bus stop with a big, strong black umbrella in his hand.
- Then are you carrying the umbrella to keep the sun off you?

Scripts

Text A   A Tall and Slim[1] Girl

At five feet six inches[2], Rosa was taller than every other student in the sixth grade[3]. She worried about[4] this all the time[5], in school and at home[6]. Her mother told her to stand up straight[7] and be proud that she was so tall and slim.

"Someday," her mother said, "you'll be happy that you're tall."

This made Rosa happier, but she was still afraid her classmates were making fun of her[8] behind her back[9]. One day, all this changed[10] when Mr. Ransom, the coach[11] from the youth club[12], asked Rosa to play center[13] in their basketball team[14]. He said that Rosa was a good basketball player and her height would make her valuable[15] as the center. Now, she really was proud to be tall. She was someone special.[16]

Text B   What a Mess!

Bill Lane has just touched[17] some wet paint[18].

Mr. Field: You mustn't[19] touch the wet paint, Bill.

Bill: I'm sorry. I won't do it again.

Mr. Field: Try to be more careful in future[20].

Bill: I shall. I wasn't as careless[21] as John Sampson. He walked across[22] that wet cement^{23} over there.

Mr. Field: The workmen^{24} oughtn't^{25} to leave it without a notice^{26}.

Bill: The headmaster had asked them to put up a notice^{27}.

Mr. Field: Then why isn't there one?

Bill: They have gone to their store to get it. Here they come^{28} with it now!

Mr. Field: But look at them! They've forgotten about^{29} the wet cement and they're walking across it to put up the notice!

Notes

1   Tall and Slim: 身材高而苗条

2   At five feet six inches: 身高 5 英尺 6 英寸

3   in the sixth grade: 在 6 年级

4   worried about: 为……担心，焦虑

5   all the time: 一直，成天

6   in school and at home: 在学校和在家里

7   stand up straight: 站直

8   were making fun of her: 取笑她

9   behind her back: 在她背后

10 all this changed: 这一切都改变了

11 the coach: 教练

12 the youth club: 青年俱乐部

13 play center: （篮球）打中锋

14 in their basketball team: 在她们篮球队中

15 valuable: 宝贵的，有价值的

16 She was someone special.: 她是与众不同的人。

17 touched: 摸，触碰

18 wet paint: 未干的油漆

19 mustn't: 不许，严禁

20 in future: 以后

21 careless: 粗心的

22 walked across: 穿过，走过

23 wet cement: 没有干的水泥地

24 The workmen: 工人

25 oughtn't: 不应该

26 leave it without a notice: 不放个告示就离开了

27 had asked them to put up a notice: 让他们放置一个告示

28 Here they come: 他们来了

29 have forgotten about: 把……给忘记了

Lesson 9

Text A

You Are Too Young to Buy Alcohol.

1 **Discuss briefly the questions with your partner.**

Have you ever celebrated for something with your friends? Share your experience with your partner.

2 **Listen to Text A once and answer the following questions.**

1 What was the conversation about?

_____

2 Where did the conversation take place?

_____

3 Why did Malc come late?

_____

3 **Listen to Text A again. Take notes and answer the questions below.**

1 Where had Steve decided to go?

_____

2 Where did Steve and others go to have a final drink?

_____

3 What did the message say?

_____

4 What competition did Malc and his friends talk about?

_____

5 Why did Malc buy drinks for all his friends?

_____

6 What did Malc order at the bar?

_____

7   Did Malc get the drinks for his friends? Why?

_____

4   **Retell the story of Text A.**

1   Form a group of three or four and retell the story together. Take turns to give sentences until the story is completed. You may choose one of the following examples as the beginning of your story.

> • Malc entered the pub, feeling pleased with himself after a successful day of photography. He shared his confidence in winning the competition with his friends.
> • Bill eagerly awaited Malc's return. When Malc arrived at the pub, he asked about Malc's experience.

2   Regroup with students from different groups in step 1. Each student retells the story from his/her previous group.

5   **Discuss the following questions in groups of three or four. After the discussion, select one member of your group to report to the class what you have talked about.**

1   Do you think it is a good idea to go to a pub for celebration? Why/Why not? What do you think is the best way to celebrate?

2   If you are going to host a celebration for your friends, how will you prepare for it?

Text B

Give Me a Big Box of Chocolates.

1   **Listen to Text B once and answer the following questions.**

1   What is the story about?

_____

2   How many people are there in the story?

_____

3   What is their relationship?

_____

2 Listen to Text B again. Take notes and answer the questions below.

1 What did John like very much?

_____

2 Did his mother give him what he liked? Why?

_____

3 Why did John's mother let him eat the chocolates his grandfather brought him?

_____

4 What was John doing one evening?

_____

5 How did John say his prayers?

_____

6 What did he want for his birthday?

_____

7 Why did John's mother go into his bedroom when she heard his prayers?

_____

8 Why did John shout his prayers?

_____

9 Where was John's grandfather that evening?

_____

10 Who do you think John was praying to?

_____

3 Describe to your partner the picture below with the following words and expressions.

in a bedroom

a bed with a spring mattress

a room decorated with pictures

hang on the wall

a picture of a puppy

a room with some toys around

a boy under ten (perhaps)

kneel at the bedside

have a sweet tooth

be crazy about chocolates

be of medium height

in the early thirties

hurry into the room

with a duster cloth in hand

be busy with household chores

be worried about

be particular about

the man at the door

look elderly

figure out what is going on

wear a puzzled look

avoid being seen

stand in the room next to the bedroom

listen with a smile

carry a big box of chocolates under one's arm

give a surprise to

play a trick on

peep at

4 Suppose you are John and your partner plays the role of John's mother. Talk why your mother never gave you any chocolates. Then talk about whether you think your mother was too strict with you and whether your grandfather loved you in the right way. Work out a solution about chocolates.

Text C

An Artist and a Farmer

1 **Read the following text aloud to your partner. Your partner listens to you without looking at the text.**

An artist went to a beautiful part of the country for a holiday, and stayed with a farmer. Every day he went out with his paints and his brushes, and painted from morning to evening, and then when it got dark, he went back to the farm and had a good dinner before he went to bed.

At the end of his holiday, he wanted to pay the farmer, but the farmer said, "No, I do not want money—but give me one of your paintings. What is money? In a week it will all be finished, but your painting will still be here."

The artist was very pleased and thanked the farmer for saying such kind things about his paintings.

The farmer smiled and answered, "I have a son in London. He wants to become an artist. When he comes here next month, I will show him your painting, and he will get some inspiration, I think."

2 **Your partner retells the story to you. Check if any information is missing in his/her retelling.**

3 **Ask your partner what occupation he/she would like to take up and why he/she wants to take up it. You can also share your answers with your partner.**

Sentence-making

Pick out useful words and expressions from the following sentences and make sentences with them.

Example

They **were bad for** his teeth.

> Smoking is bad for one's health.
> Reading in bed is bad for your eyes.
> Violence on TV is bad for children.

- He went round to the pub.
- You'd better buy us each a drink.
- You're too young to buy alcohol.
- He brought John chocolates when he came to visit him.
- His mother let him eat them.
- She wanted to make the old man happy.
- Make them give me a big box of chocolates for my birthday.
- She heard the small boy shouting.
- The clever boy answered with a smile.
- An artist went to a beautiful part of the country for a holiday.
- The artist thanked the farmer for saying such kind things about his paintings.

Scripts

Text A　You Are Too Young to Buy Alcohol.[1]

One day, Steve told the group that he had decided to go back to Edinburgh[2]. "I want to see the rest of the festival[3]," he explained. That evening, they all went to a pub for a final drink[4] with Steve. They left a message for Malc[5]: Gone to the White Pub. See you there!

Malc arrived back quite late. He went round to the pub immediately. He was feeling very pleased with himself.[6]

Bill: How did it go, then?

Malc: Oh, fantastic[7]! I took some really good photographs. I'm sure I will win that competition[8].

Lise: Well, you'd better buy us each a drink, then!

Malc: Yes...What would you all like?

Malc goes to the bar.

Malc: I'd like four pints of best bitter[9]...oh, and two lagers and lime[10].

Barman: ...Oh, excuse me, sir. How old are you?

Malc: Sixteen. Why?

Barman: Well, I'm afraid you're too young to buy alcohol. You have to be eighteen, you know.

Text B   Give Me a Big Box of Chocolates.

John liked chocolates very much, but his mother never gave him any because they were bad for his teeth[11], she thought. But John had a very nice grandfather. The old man loved his grandson very much, and sometimes he brought John chocolates when he came to visit him. Then his mother let him eat them because she wanted to make the old man happy[12].

One evening, a few days before John's seventh birthday[13], he was saying his prayers[14] in his bedroom before he went to bed. "Please, God," he shouted, "make them give me a big box of chocolates for my birthday[15] on Saturday."

His mother was in the kitchen, but she heard the small boy shouting[16] and went into his bedroom quickly.

"Why are you shouting, John?" she asked her son. "God can hear you when you talk quietly."

"I know," answered the clever boy with a smile[17], "but grandfather's in the next room, and he can't."

Notes

1   You Are Too Young to Buy Alcohol.: 你还太小，不能买酒。

2   Edinburgh: 爱丁堡，英国北部苏格兰的首府

3   the rest of the festival: 剩下的节日活动

4   went to a pub for a final drink: 到一个酒馆最后喝一杯

5　left a message for Malc: 给马尔茨留言

6　He was feeling very pleased with himself.: 他对自己极为得意。

7　fantastic: 太棒了

8　win that competition: 在比赛中获胜

9　four pints of best bitter: 四品脱最好的苦啤酒

　　pint: 度量单位

10　two lagers and lime: 两杯加酸橙的淡啤酒

11　bad for his teeth: 对他的牙齿不好

12　make the old man happy: 使老人（爷爷）高兴

13　a few days before John's seventh birthday: 在约翰 7 岁生日前几天

14　he was saying his prayers: 他正在做祈祷

15　give me a big box of chocolates for my birthday: 给我一大盒巧克力作为我的生日礼物

16　she heard the small boy shouting: 她听到这个小男孩大声喊

17　answered the clever boy with a smile: 倒装句，小男孩面带微笑地回答

Lesson 10

Text A

They Don't Talk.

1 Discuss briefly the questions with your partner.

Have you ever been angry with your roommates/classmates? What did you do?

2 Listen to Text A once and answer the following questions.

1 Where did the story take place?

_____

2 How many people were there in the story?

_____

3 What was their relationship?

_____

3 Listen to Text A again. Take notes and answer the questions below.

1 Why didn't Mr. and Mrs. Jones speak to each other for several days?

_____

2 Why did Mr. Jones go to bed soon after dinner one evening?

_____

3 Did he say anything to Mrs. Jones before he went upstairs?

_____

4 Did Mrs. Jones go to bed immediately after her husband went upstairs?

_____

5 What did Mrs. Jones do after her husband had gone upstairs?

_____

6 What did she see on the table near her bed?

_____

7 What was written on it?

_____

8   When did Mr. Jones wake up the next morning?

_____

9   What did he see on the small table near his bed?

_____

10   What was written on it?

_____

11   Do you think Mr. and Mrs. Jones did the right thing? Explain.

_____

4 **Retell the story of Text A.**

1   Form a group of three or four and retell the story together. Take turns to give sentences until the story is completed. You may choose one of the following examples as the beginning of your story.

> • I was very angry with my husband, and he was very angry with me. So for several days, we didn't speak to each other.
> • One day, I quarreled with my wife. I was so angry with her that I didn't speak to her for several days.
> • One morning, Mr. Jones had to get up early. So he wanted his wife to wake him up at 7 a.m.

2   Regroup with students from different groups in step 1. Each student retells the story from his/her previous group.

5 **Discuss the following questions in groups of three or four. After the discussion, select one member of your group to report to the class what you have talked about.**

1   Use as many descriptive words as you can to describe Mr. and Mrs. Jones.
2   Do you think Mr. Jones would be even angrier with his wife? Why?
3   What do you think would be the right way for Mr. Jones to ask for help from his wife?

Text B

A Dirty Car

1 **Listen to Text B once and answer the following questions.**

1   How many people are involved in this dialogue? What are they talking about?

_____

2   Do they usually clean the car together?

_____

3   What is their relationship?

_____

2 **Listen to Text B again. Take notes and answer the questions below.**

1   Whose car is it? Who usually clean the car?

_____

2   Why is the car very dirty?

_____

3   Who are standing near the car?

_____

4   Did they clean the car a couple of days ago? Do they decide to clean the car today?

_____

5   Who does Peter think should clean the car? Why?

_____

6   Whose turn is it according to John? Why?

_____

7   How do the boys take turns?

_____

8   When is John going to clean the car?

_____

9   Why does he put it off again?

_____

10   Do you think John is lazy?

_____

3 Describe to your partner the picture below with the following words and expressions.

three boys
in their teens
dark curly hair
be casually dressed
in shorts
a pair of rain boots
a pullover
with their hands in their pockets
a car parked on the wet road
with mud stains all over the car
look at
talk to
seem to be arguing over sth.
a lot of space near where they live

4 Suppose you are John and your partner plays the role of Peter. How do you reply when Peter says you are lazy for putting off cleaning the car?

Text C

The Garden Work

1 **Read the following text aloud to your partner. Your partner listens to you without looking at the text.**

> Ellen walked briskly out into the garden and took a deep breath of cool, fresh air. She was eager to begin work. This time of year, with new growth everywhere, always made her feel that she had to help things grow. She gathered her tools, went to the patch of freshly turned earth and began to dig rows of holes. Then she carefully picked up one plant and placed it in a hole. Over and over, she performed this same task and then gently patted the earth around each plant. Her growling stomach and the sun high overhead told her that it was time to take a break.

2 **Your partner retells the story to you. Check if any information is missing in his/her retelling.**

3 **Ask your partner if he/she prefers to work outdoors or indoors and why. You can also share with your partner your opinion, starting with your agreement or disagreement with your partner's opinion.**

Sentence-making

Pick out useful words and expressions from the following sentences and make sentences with them.

Example

Mr. Jones **was** very **angry with** his wife.

▷ His wife was so angry with him that she gave him a push.

▷ "Don't be angry with me, please," he pleaded.

- For several days, they did not speak to each other.
- He went to bed soon after dinner.
- Mrs. Jones washed the dinner things and then did some reading.
- Mrs. Jones went to bed much later than her husband.
- When Mr. Jones woke up the next morning, it was nearly 8 a.m.
- The car hasn't been cleaned for a few days.
- Someone ought to clean it today.
- It's his turn.
- You always clean it after Mark.
- You should enjoy working.
- She was eager to begin work.
- Over and over, she performed this same task and then gently patted the earth around each plant.

Scripts

Text A   They Don't Talk.

Mr. Jones was very angry with[1] his wife, and she was very angry with her husband. For several days[2], they did not speak to each other[3] at all. One evening, Mr. Jones was very tired[4] when he came back from work, so he went to bed soon after dinner[5]. Of course, he did not say anything to Mrs. Jones before he went upstairs. Mrs. Jones washed the dinner things[6] and then did some reading[7].

When she went to bed much later than her husband[8], she found a piece of paper on the small table near her bed. On it were the words[9]: "Mother.—Wake me up at 7 a.m.[10]—Father."

When Mr. Jones woke up the next morning, it was nearly 8 a.m.[11], and on the small table near his bed, he saw another piece of paper. He took it and read these words[12]: "Father.—Wake up. It is 7 a.m.—Mother."

Text B   A Dirty Car

John, Peter and Mark are brothers. Their father has a new car, and they clean it for him. It has just rained, and the car is very dirty. John is looking at it, and he is talking to Peter.

John: The car hasn't been cleaned for a few days.

Peter: No, it hasn't. It's very dirty.

John: Someone ought to[13] clean it today.

Peter: Mark should clean it. It's his turn.[14]

John: No, he cleaned it last time. It's your turn.

Peter: No, it isn't. You always clean it after Mark.[15]

John: Oh dear, is it really my turn? In that case[16], I'll clean it tomorrow.

Peter: Clean it now. Only lazy people[17] say they'll work tomorrow.

John: Then I'll clean it the day after tomorrow[18].

Peter: You are lazy. You ought to be ashamed.[19] You should enjoy working[20].

Notes

1   was very angry with: 对……非常生气

2   For several days: 几天来

3   did not speak to each other: （他们之间）互不讲话

4   was very tired: 非常疲倦

5   went to bed soon after dinner: 晚饭后不久就去睡觉了

6   the dinner things: 晚饭用的餐具

7   did some reading: 看了一会儿书

8   she went to bed much later than her husband: 她睡觉比她丈夫晚得多

9   On it were the words: 上面写着这些字

10   Wake me up at 7 a.m.: 7 点钟叫醒我。

11   it was nearly 8 a.m.: 都快 8 点了

12   read these words: 看到了这句话

13   ought to: 应该

14   It's his turn.: 该轮到他了。

15   You always clean it after Mark.: 马克擦过后总是轮到你擦车。

16   In that case: 如果是那样的话

17   lazy people: 懒惰的人

18   the day after tomorrow: 后天

19   You ought to be ashamed.: 你应该感到害臊。

20   enjoy working: 喜欢工作

Lesson 11

Text A

I'll Start in Three Months' Time.

1 **Discuss briefly the questions with your partner.**

Have you ever had an interview? What questions will you ask the employer if you are interviewed for a job?

2 **Listen to Text A once and answer the following questions.**

1 What is the story about?

_____

2 How old was Rose?

_____

3 What did she do after she left high school?

_____

3 **Listen to Text A again. Take notes and answer the questions below.**

1 What did Rose learn at college?

_____

2 Was Rose a good student? How do you know?

_____

3 Where did she live?

_____

4 Was it easy for her to find interesting work? Why?

_____

5 Which office did Rose choose?

_____

6 Why did she choose this office?

_____

7   What did she say to the manager of the office?

_____

8   How much would they pay her?

_____

9   Would Rose start working right away? Why not?

_____

10 Do you think Rose could get 450 dollars a week if she started in three
    months' time? Why?

_____

4 **Retell the story of Text A.**

1   Form a group of three or four and retell the story together. Take turns to give
    sentences until the story is completed. You may choose one of the following
    examples as the beginning of your story.

> • Rose was twenty-one years old. She wanted to be economically
>   independent.
> • I was seventeen years old when I left high school. Then I learned computer
>   programming at college for four years.
> • Rose was looking for work for the first time. She didn't know much about
>   how to get a job.

2   Regroup with students from different groups in step 1. Each student retells
    the story from his/her previous group.

5 **Discuss the following questions in groups of three or four. After the
discussion, select one member of your group to report to the class what you
have talked about.**

1   Would you hire Rose if you were the manager of the office? Why?
2   What advice would you give Rose to help her find a job?
3   What job would you like to do when you graduate? Why?

Text B

I'll Find My Way.

1 **Listen to Text B once and answer the following questions.**

1　What is the dialogue about?

2　What is Uncle George doing?

3　What are Mrs. Miller and Mary doing when Uncle George calls?

2 **Listen to Text B again. Take notes and answer the questions below.**

1　Who answers the phone?

2　What is the relationship between Mary and Mrs. Miller?

3　Where is Uncle George?

4　What does Mrs. Miller offer to do?

5　What do you think is the relationship between Mrs. Miller and Michael?

6　Does Uncle George want Michael to meet him? Why not?

7　Where does Mrs. Miller live?

8　How will Uncle George get to Mrs. Miller's house?

9　Who has set the table?

10　Will Uncle George get lost again?

3 Describe to your partner the picture below with the following words and expressions.

a sunny day
a man talking on his mobile phone
call sb.
speak into the phone
try very hard to explain sth.
look worried
in his mid-forties
wear a pair of glasses
be dressed in a dark suit
a big square
a white car parked at the roadside
look like a new car
wait for him inside the car
a large statue
in the street
take a walk
ride a bike
go somewhere
two lampposts

4 Suppose you are your partner's uncle/aunt and are coming to visit him/her. About a couple of blocks away from his/her dormitory, you start to call for specific directions. Make a conversation.

Text C

A Break in the Routine

1 Read the section with the marks "*" below aloud to your partner. Your partner listens to you without looking at the text.

Jonathan Rivers lived alone in a neat, two-storey, semi-detached house in Compton Street. Like many bachelors approaching middle age, he was getting rather set in his ways. He caught the same train to London every morning, ate his lunch in the same crowded restaurant near the office where he worked and always came home on the 6:00 train. People were so used to seeing Jonathan set off at a quarter past eight, dressed in a simple dark suit, wearing a black bowler hat and carrying a rolled umbrella on his arm, that they said you didn't need to wear a watch if you lived in Compton Street.

Ever since Jonathan had set up house in Compton Street, he had looked after it very carefully. He worked hard in the garden every Sunday and set out to impress the neighbors with his flower beds and lawn. Before he left the house in the mornings, he carefully closed all the doors downstairs, opened some windows to let the air in and locked the front door. Everything Jonathan did was tidy and systematic.

*One summer evening, Jonathan returned home as usual at five minutes to seven precisely. When he opened the front gate, he immediately noticed something strange.

There was a heavy footprint in the earth in one of the flower beds. Jonathan was just going to blame the milkman or the courier when he noticed that one of the white lace curtains in the front room downstairs was out of place. Jonathan never left anything out of place.

He walked to the front door and opened it quietly. He listened carefully for a few moments but could hear nothing. The front-room door was half-open. Jonathan studied it thoughtfully, wondering if he had forgotten to close it that morning. He had never forgotten before. He stepped silently across the hall to the door and looked inside the room. The shadow of a man was clearly reflected on the far wall in the evening sunlight. He had obviously been standing behind the door since Jonathan's return. Jonathan grabbed the door handle, slammed the door and turned the key. Then he calmly took his cellphone from his pocket and set about calling the police.*

The burglar, a tall, thick-set, bearded fellow, tried to climb through a window to get out but Jonathan had expected that. He set about stabbing him with his umbrella, using it like a sword. Three minutes later, the police arrived on the scene. Jonathan was a little annoyed that he had to have dinner later than usual but on the whole, he felt quite pleased with himself.

2 **Your partner retells what he/she has heard. Check if any information is missing in his/her retelling.**

3 **Ask your partner to tell you what he/she does on an average day. Then you tell your partner what you do on an average day.**

Sentence-making

Pick out useful words and expressions from the following sentences and make sentences with them.

Example

We're **in the middle of** the block.

> They were in the middle of a meeting when the news arrived.
> She stopped him in the middle of his speech.

- She passed her examinations quite well.
- A lot of companies were looking for computer programmers.
- So it was not difficult to find interesting work.
- I won't need to go by bus.
- We'll pay you 380 dollars a week now.
- Rose thought for a few seconds before she answered.

- The day of Uncle George's arrival is here.
- Uncle George can't find his way to the Miller's.
- Mrs. Miller gives him specific directions on the phone.
- Is the table set?
- Like many bachelors approaching middle age, he was getting rather set in his ways.
- Jonathan returned home as usual at five minutes to seven precisely.
- Jonathan never left anything out of place.
- Then he set about calling the police.

Scripts

Text A　I'll Start in Three Months' Time.[1]

Rose left high school[2] when she was seventeen and went to college to learn computer programming[3]. She passed her examinations quite well[4] at college. After four years of study, she graduated and then went to look for work[5]. She was still living with her parents.

A lot of companies were looking for computer programmers[6], so it was not difficult to find interesting work. Rose went to several offices[7], and then chose one of them. It was near her parents' house. She thought, "I'll walk there every morning. I won't need to go by bus[8]."

She went to the office again and said to the manager, "I want to work here, but what will you pay me[9]?"

"We'll pay you 380 dollars a week[10] now," the manager answered, "and 450 dollars a week after three months[11]."

Rose thought for a few seconds[12] before she answered. Then she said, "All right, then I'll start in three months' time."

Text B　I'll Find My Way.[13]

The day of Uncle George's arrival is here.[14] Everything is ready, but Uncle George and his family haven't arrived. Uncle George can't find his way to[15] the Miller's. Mrs. Miller gives him specific directions[16] on the phone[17].

Mrs. Miller:	Please answer my phone[18], Mary.
Mary:	Hello, Uncle George? Where are you? Wait a minute, please. I'll call my mother. Mother, it's Uncle George.
Mrs. Miller:	George, dear. Where are you? At the corner of Pine and State Street?[19] Wait there. Michael can go and get you[20].
Uncle George:	No. It's not necessary. We drive the car. Give me the directions.[21] I'll find my way.
Mrs. Miller:	Go north on State Street to Main Street. There's a large statue[22] there. Turn left.[23] Continue to[24] Grove Avenue. Turn right. Continue on Grove Avenue to Seventh Street. Turn left. We're in the middle of the block[25]. Can you repeat the directions, George?
Uncle George:	I think so. I have to go north on State Street to Main Street. I turn left to Grove Avenue. I continue on Grove Avenue. I turn right. I continue on Grove Avenue to Seventh Street. I turn left and go to the middle of the block.
Mrs. Miller:	That's it.[26] I'll see you soon, George. Mary, is the table set[27]?
Mary:	Yes, Mother. Come and look.
Mrs. Miller:	It looks very pretty. Thank you, Mary.

Notes

1   I'll Start in Three Months' Time.: 我三个月后再开始工作。

2   left high school: 离开高中，高中毕业

3   learn computer programming: 学习计算机编程

4   passed her examinations quite well: 以较好的成绩通过考试

5   look for work: 找工作

6   computer programmers: 计算机程序员

7   offices: 公司办公室，事务所

8   go by bus: 乘公共汽车去

9   but what will you pay me: 不过你给我多少薪水

10   pay you 380 dollars a week: 每周付给你 380 美元

11   450 dollars a week after three months: 三个月后每周付给你 450 美元

12   thought for a few seconds: 想了一会儿

13   I'll Find My Way.: 我会认路的。/ 我会知道怎么走的。

14   The day of Uncle George's arrival is here.: 乔治叔叔该来的那天到了。

15   find his way to: 找到去……的路

16   gives him specific directions: 给他仔细地指示方向

17   on the phone: 在电话上

18   answer my phone: 替我接电话

19   At the corner of Pine and State Street?: 在松树和州大街相交的街角？

20 go and get you: 去接你

21 Give me the directions.: 告诉我怎么走。

22 statue: 雕像

23 Turn left.: 向左转弯。

24 Continue to: 继续（走到）

25 in the middle of the block: 在街区的中央

26 That's it.: 对了。

27 is the table set: 摆好桌子了吗

Lesson 12

Text A

The Charcoal Pit

1 Discuss briefly the questions with your partner.

Are there any restaurants you like very much? Describe one of them and explain why.

2 Listen to Text A once and answer the following questions.

1 What is the story about?

2 What business did Erika do?

3 Was Erika's business going well?

3 Listen to Text A again. Take notes and answer the questions below.

1 Was Erika's restaurant a new one?

2 Why was Erika worried?

3 What was Erika's problem?

4 How was the business of the new restaurant across the street?

5 What did Erika notice about the new restaurant?

6 What was Erika going to do?

7   What was Erika thinking about?

_____

8   What were the possible ways that Erika had thought of to solve the problem?

_____

4 **Retell the story of Text A.**

1   Form a group of three or four and retell the story together. Take turns to give sentences until the story is completed. You may choose one of the following examples as the beginning of your story.

> - I have a restaurant. Business had been very good until last month when a new restaurant opened right across the street.
> - Erika was thinking hard. She wanted to make her restaurant the best one in town.
> - There are two restaurants close to my house, across the street from each other. One of them is new, the other has been there for many years.

2   Regroup with students from different groups in step 1. Each student retells the story from his/her previous group.

5 **Discuss the following questions in groups of three or four. After the discussion, select one member of your group to report to the class what you have talked about.**

1   What do you suggest that Erika do in order to make her restaurant the most popular one in town?

2   Which restaurant will you choose if you are dining out with friends, an expensive restaurant with beautiful surroundings or a cheap restaurant with delicious food? Why?

Text B

There Is Hope for Us!

1 **Listen to Text B once and answer the following questions.**

1   What is the dialogue about?

_____

2   Where are the girls?

_____

3   What are they talking about?

_____

2   **Listen to Text B again. Take notes and answer the questions below.**

1   They have not danced for a long time, have they?

_____

2   What does Tina think they have to do? Why?

_____

3   What have they been doing respectively since they last saw each other?

_____

4   Why does Leela learn Japanese every evening?

_____

5   What are they going to do?

_____

6   Where are they going? Why are they going there?

_____

7   Do you think there is a good dance teacher in the dance hall? Why do you think so?

_____

3   **Describe to your partner the picture below with the following words and expressions.**

at the weekend

in a dance hall

the students' union

hold a party

full of people

in skirts

wear ties

permed hair

straight hair

the couple in front

at the back

in high spirits

musicians on the platform

musical instruments

a band of five

play the music

play the violin/clarinet

with great enthusiasm

enjoy what they are doing

4 Suppose you are Tina and your partner plays the role of Leela. Discuss what you will do when you have finished the dancing lesson.

Text C

The Snow in the Morning

1 Read the following text aloud to your partner. Your partner listens to you without looking at the text.

When I looked out of the window and saw the snow drift in the driveway, I thought to myself that I should never have gotten out of bed. I had been making preparations for more than two days for a large dinner party to be held that night and knew that several of the people I was expecting to come would be calling to cancel if the snow continued much longer. I called upstairs to tell Jerry to look out of the window. Jerry heard me and quickly got out of bed. He knew that the weather forecaster had been predicting snow. Now it had really come. To Jerry, two or three inches of fresh snow would be just what was needed to make the ski trip a big success.

2 Your partner retells the story to you. Check if any information is missing in his/her retelling.

3 Ask your partner what he/she thinks a good winter sport is and why. You can also share with your partner your opinion and reason.

Sentence-making

Pick out useful words and expressions from the following sentences and make sentences with them.

Example

What **was** she **going to** do?

➢ What are you going to do after school?

➢ Are you going to do shopping this weekend?

➢ What are you going to have for lunch?

- The new restaurant across the street now had more customers.
- She had even seen some of her own customers going to eat at the Charcoal Pit.
- One thing she could do was to revise her menu.
- She might add omelets and casseroles.
- This will certainly lift her spirits.
- Erika would fight to make her restaurant the most popular one in town.
- He could give her some new ideas.
- Tina and Leela are talking to each other.
- They are standing outside a dance hall.
- —I haven't danced for a long time. —Neither have I.
- We must go to a dance soon, or we'll forget how to dance.

- What have you been doing since I last saw you?
- We'll both have to start learning all the new dances.
- I thought to myself that I should never have gotten out of bed.
- To Jerry, two or three inches of fresh snow would be just what was needed to make the ski trip a big success.

Scripts

Text A   The Charcoal Pit[1]

Erika was worried. Her restaurant was losing customers. The new restaurant across the street[2] now had more customers than she did. She had even seen some of her own customers going to eat at the Charcoal Pit. What was she going to do?

One thing she could do was to revise her menu.[3] Maybe not everyone wanted hamburgers[4]. She might add omelets and casseroles[5]. The menu might help.

Perhaps the decor of her restaurant was dated[6]. She could redecorate[7] the place. Erika decided to consult an interior decorator[8] who could give her some new ideas. A facelift for Burger Haven would certainly lift her spirits.[9]

In fact, she felt better after thinking of some improvements. Erika would fight to make her restaurant the most popular one in town.

Text B   There Is Hope for Us!

Tina and Leela are talking to each other. They are standing outside a dance hall and they are talking about dancing.

Tina: I haven't danced for a long time.
Leela: Neither have I.
Tina: We must go to a dance soon, or we'll forget how to dance[10].
Leela: Yes, we must. What have you been doing since I last saw you?
Tina: I've been studying hard for my examinations. And you?
Leela: I've been learning Japanese every evening.
Tina: Why have you been learning Japanese? Why not English?[11]
Leela: I hope to visit Japan next year.
Tina: Well, we'll both have to start learning all the new dances.

Leela: Yes, let's go into the dance hall and ask if we can take dancing lessons[12].

Tina: A good idea. They can teach elephants to dance nowadays: Perhaps there's hope for us![13]

Notes

1   The Charcoal Pit: 街对面新开饭馆的店名

2   across the street: 在街对面

3   One thing she could do was to revise her menu.: 有一件事她能做，就是调整她的菜单。

4   hamburgers: 汉堡包

5   omelets and casseroles: 煎蛋饼和砂锅菜

6   the decor of her restaurant was dated: （也许）她饭馆的内部装饰过时了

7   redecorate: 重新装修

8   consult an interior decorator: 向一位室内装饰师咨询

9   A facelift for Burger Haven would certainly lift her spirits.: 给她的饭馆（Burger Haven）整修一番，肯定能振奋她的精神。

10 or we'll forget how to dance: 不然，我们会忘记怎么跳舞了

11 Why not English?: 你为什么不学习英语？

12 take dancing lessons: 去一个舞蹈班上课

13 Perhaps there's hope for us!: 我们也许还有希望（学会跳舞）！

Lesson 13

Text A

The Country Schoolhouse

1 Discuss briefly the questions with your partner.

Have you ever had a hard time with your classmates in primary or secondary school? Can you share your story?

2 Listen to Text A once and answer the following questions.

1 What is this text about?

2 Was it a regular school the boy attended?

3 Did the boy have a good beginning at the school?

3 Listen to Text A again. Take notes and answer the questions below.

1 How far was the school from the farm?

2 Where was the school?

3 How many students would the schoolhouse hold?

4 How often did they attend the school in summer?

5 How did they go to the school?

6 How did they bring their dinners?

7   What did they usually have for dinner?

_____

8   Where did they have their dinners?

_____

9   When did the boy make his first visit to the school?

_____

10   Who stopped the boy at the school?

_____

11   What did the girl look like?

_____

12   What did the girl tell the crowd about the boy?

_____

13   Why did the boy feel embarrassed?

_____

14   Who saved the boy from the embarrassment? What did she do?

_____

15   Do you think the boy would be afraid of being different after this incident? Why?

_____

4 **Retell the story of Text A.**

1   Form a group of three or four and retell the story together. Take turns to give sentences until the story is completed. You may choose one of the following examples as the beginning of your story.

> • My first visit to the school was not very pleasant. I was seven years old at that time.
> • The country schoolhouse was the most delightful place in my childhood. It was not big.
> • In the village where I lived, no child at the age of seven wore glasses. But the new boy was an exception.

2   Regroup with students from different groups in step 1. Each student retells the story from his/her previous group.

5 **Discuss the following questions in groups of three or four. After the discussion, select one member of your group to report to the class what you have talked about.**

1   Use as many descriptive words as you can to describe the boy's school life.

2 Do you think children who are different from others tend to have a hard time
   in school? Why?
3 Have you ever helped a friend or a classmate who was in public embarrassment?
   What did you do?

Text B

On a Camping Holiday

1 **Listen to Text B once and answer the following questions.**

1 How many people are there in the dialogue? What is their relationship?

_____

2 What are they talking about?

_____

3 Is it their first day on holiday? Why?

_____

2 **Listen to Text B again. Take notes and answer the questions below.**

1 Have the boys brought a lot of food with them?

_____

2 Who is hungry?

_____

3 Have they got much rice left?

_____

4 Have they got any potatoes?

_____

5 What do they have at the moment?

_____

6 What else does Jimmy want to eat?

_____

7 Where can they get more food? How will they get there?

_____

8 Who will get food in the village and who will cook the meat?

_____

3 **Describe to your partner the picture below with the following words and expressions.**

a camping site

a fence in the distance

distant hills

branches of an old tree

a tent big enough for two people

set up in the shade of the tree

a sleeping bag inside the tent

a knapsack on the grass in front of the tent

a pan with a long handle

two mugs

a portable stove

two teenagers

stand between the stove and the knapsack

be dressed in a sweater and a pair of jeans

wear a pair of sneakers

hold a frying pan and half a loaf of bread

in his right/left hand

look at

kneel on the grass

hold a tin in his right hand

a little rice in the tin

> not enough for a meal
> hold the lid of the tin
> speak to
> wear a pullover

4 **Suppose you are Jimmy and your partner is Donald. Talk about making preparations for a picnic at the weekend.**

Text C

A Depressing Film

1 **Play the audio of the following text to your partner. Your partner listens without looking at the text.**

Peter: Hello, Jim. What was the film like?

Jim: Awful. It was a complete waste of time.

Peter: Why? What was it about?

Jim: It was about a married couple. They had to live with the wife's mother because they didn't have enough money to buy a house of their own.

Peter: A lot of young people have to do that.

Jim: Yes, but the husband had to work overtime three times a week, so he was always tired.

Peter: It sounds like the story of my life.

Jim: Yes, it does. But this man was always overtired, and he couldn't sleep. So he used to take two sleeping pills every night.

Peter: I take sleeping pills sometimes.

Jim: Yes, but not two every night. Anyway, the strain was too much for him. He had a nervous breakdown and had to go to hospital.

Peter: It sounds like a very depressing film.

Jim: Not really. His wife was able to find a good job as an interpreter because she could speak French and German fluently. After a few months' work, she had a better job than her husband. So in the end, they were able to buy a house.

Peter: My wife used to speak French. I must tell her to brush it up.

2 Your partner retells what the conversation is about. Check if any information is missing in his/her retelling.

3 Ask your partner what films he/she likes and why. You can also tell your partner what films you like and give an example.

Sentence-making

Pick out useful words and expressions from the following sentences and make sentences with them.

Example

The country schoolhouse **was three miles from** my uncle's farm.

- ➤ The new theater is only a few hundred meters from our school.
- ➤ My father's office is five kilometers from our house.
- ➤ The only hospital in this area was 20 miles from our village.

- It would hold about twenty-five boys and girls.
- We attended the school with more or less regularity once or twice a week in summer.
- We sat in the shade of the trees at noon.
- It is the part of my education which I look back upon with the most satisfaction.
- My first visit to the school was when I was seven.
- It roused her scorn.
- She reported me to all the crowd.
- Here is a boy of seven years old who can't see clearly without glasses.
- I was the only one who wore glasses.
- I was about to take off my glasses.
- Jimmy Booth and Donald Black are on a camping holiday.
- They have brought only a little food with them.
- It was a complete waste of time.
- It sounds like the story of my life.

Scripts

Text A　The Country Schoolhouse[1]

The country schoolhouse was three miles from my uncle's farm. It stood in a clearing in the woods[2] and would hold[3] about twenty-five boys and girls. We attended the school[4] with more or less regularity[5] once or twice a week in summer. We walked to it in the cool of the morning[6] by the forest paths, and back in the dusk[7] at the end of the day. All the pupils brought their dinners in baskets—corn dodger[8], buttermilk[9], and other good things. We sat in the shade of the trees[10] at noon[11] and ate them. It is the part of my education which I look back upon[12] with the most satisfaction[13].

My first visit to the school was when I was seven, and it did not start well[14]. A strapping girl of eight[15], in the customary sunbonnet and calico dress[16], stopped me and asked about my glasses. I told her they helped to correct my short-sightedness[17]. It roused her scorn[18]. She reported me to[19] all the crowd, and said: "Here is a boy of seven years old who can't see clearly without glasses[20]." By the looks and comments which this produced[21], I realized that I was the only one who wore glasses. I was ashamed of myself[22] and about to take off my glasses when another girl, slightly taller[23] than I was, came up and said: "My brother wears glasses, too. I think he looks cute and clever. You are also handsome and clever with glasses." I looked at her through my glasses. She was the most beautiful girl I had ever seen. And I thought I was the most handsome boy in the school.

Text B　On a Camping Holiday[24]

Jimmy Booth and Donald Black are on a camping holiday. They have brought only a little food with them. Jimmy is hungry and he is looking at some rice in a tin[25]. There is only a little rice in the tin.

Jimmy:　There isn't much rice, is there?
Donald:　No, there isn't, but there are some vegetables.
Jimmy:　Are there any potatoes?
Donald:　No, there aren't. I'm sorry.
Jimmy:　I'm very hungry, Donald. What can I eat?
Donald:　There's a little bread and there are a few biscuits[26].
Jimmy:　But I want some rice and some meat.
Donald:　All right, I'll walk to the village[27] and I'll get some meat.

Jimmy: Good. By the way²⁸, who's going to cook the meat?
Donald: You'll cook it of course!

Notes

1   Schoolhouse: 校舍
2   a clearing in the woods: 树林中的一块空地
3   hold: 容纳
4   attended the school: 上学
5   with more or less regularity: 多少有些规律
6   in the cool of the morning: 在凉爽的早晨
7   in the dusk: 黄昏时
8   corn dodger: 玉米饼
9   buttermilk: 脱脂牛奶
10   in the shade of the trees: 在树阴下
11   at noon: 在中午
12   look back upon: 回顾
13   with the most satisfaction: 怀着极大的满足感
14   it did not start well: 开始不是很顺利
15   A strapping girl of eight: 一个身材高大的 8 岁女孩
16   in the customary sunbonnet and calico dress: 戴着普通的太阳帽，穿着印花布连衣裙
17   they helped to correct my short-sightedness: 眼镜能帮助我矫正近视
18   roused her scorn: 激起了她的蔑视
19   reported me to: 向……告发了我
20   can't see clearly without glasses: 不戴眼镜就看不清东西
21   the looks and comments which this produced:（她的话）引起（围观同学的）各种表情和议论
22   ashamed of myself: 为我自己感到羞愧
23   slightly taller: 稍微高一点儿
24   On a Camping Holiday: 野营度假
25   in a tin: 在罐子里
26   biscuits: 饼干
27   walk to the village: 走到村子去
28   By the way: 顺便说一下

Lesson 14

Text A

What's Going On Here?

1 **Discuss briefly the questions with your partner.**

How can you tell whether someone is lying? Share your methods with your partner.

2 **Listen to Text A once and answer the following questions.**

1 How many people are there in the conversation?

_____

2 Who are they?

_____

3 Where do you think the conversation takes place?

_____

3 **Listen to Text A again. Take notes and answer the questions below.**

1 What is the man doing?

_____

2 Why is the man doing that?

_____

3 Whose house is it?

_____

4 What is Fred doing?

_____

5 What does the policeman think is strange about the two men?

_____

6 How does the man explain himself?

_____

7   Does the policeman believe him?

_____

8   Is the man's brother at home? Why?

_____

4   **Retell the story of Text A.**

1   Form a group of three or four and retell the story together. Take turns to give sentences until the story is completed. You may choose one of the following examples as the beginning of your story.

> • The policeman arrived at the scene and asked why the man was trying to climb out of the window.
> • Outside a house, a man was explaining to a policeman that he was trying to climb out of the window with Fred's help.

2   Regroup with students from different groups in step 1. Each student retells the story from his/her previous group.

5   **Discuss the following questions in groups of three or four. After the discussion, select one member of your group to report to the class what you have talked about.**

1   Do you think the man is telling the truth? What do you think they are doing?
2   What should the policeman do?

Text B

A Lesson to Learn

1   **Listen to Text B once and answer the following questions.**

1   What is the story about?

_____

2   How many people are there in the story? What is their relationship?

_____

2 Listen to Text B again. Take notes and answer the questions below.

1   What did John do every morning?

_____

2   How did he go to school?

_____

3   What did his father tell him one day?

_____

4   When and where did his father have to go the next day?

_____

5   Did John's mother have a car of her own?

_____

6   Could she take John to school by her car?

_____

7   What would she be doing at the time when John had to leave the house?

_____

8   What did John's father suggest?

_____

9   Why did John's father want John to go to school by taxi?

_____

10 What do you think the point of the story is?

_____

3 Describe to your partner the picture below with the following words and expressions.

a very big house with large windows

look like a two-storey mansion

a owner of the house

spacious

trees in the garden

tall pine trees

a taxi in front of the house

a man wearing a hat

open the door for the boy

a little boy with a schoolbag under his arm

a taxi driver

smile politely

4 Suppose you are John and your partner is John's father. Talk with your partner whether you would learn a good lesson by going to school by taxi and give your reason. Then talk with your partner what is the best means of transportation for school-going kids and give your reason.

Text C

A Pair of Stilts

1 Read the following text aloud to your partner. Your partner listens to you without looking at the text.

Todd heard all the hammering behind the Marsey's house. He went to see what was going on. Jeff Marsey was making something from long pieces of wood.

"What is it?" Todd asked.

"A pair of stilts," Jeff said.

Todd knew that stilts could make Jeff several feet taller. Jeff was putting blocks of wood on the stilts. These were for his feet to rest on. Once Jeff got used to them, he could walk anywhere on stilts.

"I'm also making a pair of long pants," Jeff said. "They'll come all the way down and cover the stilts. I'll look like a giant."

As the summer went on, Todd forgot all about the stilts.

One night, Todd was watching television. His cousin came running in the front door. He'd never seen her so excited.

"You'd better call the police," she said.

"Why?" asked Todd.

"I was walking home," she said. "I looked up and saw a—a giant. He was following me. He wore big baggy pants. He was very stiff and straight. Each step was a huge step. I'm going to call the police."

"Wait," said Todd. "It wasn't a giant. You'll be surprised when I tell you who it was!"

2 **Your partner retells the story to you. Check if any information is missing in his/her retelling.**

3 **Ask your partner to talk about one of the things he/she has made and how it was made. You can also share with your partner your experience of making things by yourself.**

Sentence-making

Pick out useful words and expressions from the following sentences and make sentences with them.

Example

The chauffeur **took** John's father **to** his office.

➤ Bus No. 332 will take you to the zoo.
➤ Derek takes his son to the cinema once a month.
➤ Last week, Mrs. Bates took her class to the garden.

- What's going on here?
- You mean, what's happening?
- He is leaving by the front door.

- I'm in a hurry.
- I don't think you're telling me the truth.
- I'm staying with him for a while.
- He's in jail for housebreaking at the moment.
- He had to go to the airport the next morning.
- He would need the car at the time when John had to go to school.
- How will I get to school if you need your car and Mummy is still in bed?
- This was a good opportunity to teach him a lesson.
- How hard life was for the less fortunate people.
- You'll go in the same way as every other child in the world.
- Jeff Marsey was making something from long pieces of wood.
- As the summer went on, Todd forgot all about the stilts.

Scripts

Text A   What's Going On Here?[1]

Policeman: What's going on here?

Man: You mean, what's happening? Well, Constable, I'm trying to get out of the window and Fred here is helping me.

Policeman: Why are you climbing through the window[2] and not leaving by the front door?

Man: Well, you see I can't find the key and I'm in a hurry. Come on, Fred, we're wasting time[3].

Policeman: Just a minute, you two. I don't think you're telling me the truth. This isn't your house, is it?[4]

Man: No, it's my brother's. I'm staying with him for a while[5].

Policeman: Is he at home?

Man: I'm afraid not. He's in jail[6] for housebreaking[7] at the moment.

Text B   A Lesson to Learn

John was the son of a wealthy businessman. Usually he was taken to school by the chauffeur[8] in his father's beautiful car[9] before the chauffeur took John's father to his office. One evening, John's father told him that he had to go to the airport early the next day[10], so he would need the car at the time when John had to go to school. He said that John's mother, who had the other car of the family[11], would still be in bed at the time John had to leave the house[12].

　　"Well, how will I get to school if you need your car and Mummy is still in bed?" John asked. His father thought this was a good opportunity to teach him a lesson[13] about how hard life was for the less fortunate people of the world[14], so he answered, "You'll go in the same way as every other child in the world[15]—by taxi."

Notes

1　What's Going On Here?: 这儿发生什么事了？/ 你们在干什么？

2　climbing through the window: 从窗户里爬出来

3　wasting time: 浪费时间

4　This isn't your house, is it?: 这不是你的房子，是吧？

5　staying with him for a while: 与他一起小住一段时间

6　in jail: 在监狱里

7　housebreaking: 入室行窃

8　was taken to school by the chauffeur: 由司机送（他）去上学

9　in his father's beautiful car: 坐他父亲那辆漂亮的汽车

10　early the next day: 翌日一清早

11　had the other car of the family: 开着家里的另一辆车

12　had to leave the house: 得离开家，得从家里出发

13　a good opportunity to teach him a lesson: 一次教育他的好机会

14　the less fortunate people of the world: 世界上不那么幸运的人

15　in the same way as every other child in the world: 跟世界上其他所有孩子一样

Lesson 15

Text A

The Honesty

1 **Discuss briefly the questions with your partner.**

Has someone ever lied to you? Can you tell your classmates what happened?

2 **Listen to Text A once and answer the following questions.**

1   What is the story about?

_____

2   Where did the story take place?

_____

3   How many people are there in the story? What is their relationship?

_____

3 **Listen to Text A again. Take notes and answer the questions below.**

1   Why did the man go there?

_____

2   Who talked with the man?

_____

3   What question did the manager ask?

_____

4   How did the man answer the question?

_____

5   What did the manager say to the man then?

_____

6   How did the man feel?

_____

7   What did a clerk say to the man?

_____

8　What advice did the clerk give to the man?

_____

9　What did the man do then?

_____

10　Who talked with the man this time and what question did he ask the man?

_____

11　How did the man answer the question?

_____

12　Do you think the insurance company will sell life insurance to the man? Why?

_____

13　Do you think the clerk should be fired? Why?

_____

4　Retell the story of Text A.

1　Form a group of three or four and retell the story together. Take turns to give sentences until the story is completed. You may choose one of the following examples as the beginning of your story.

- A friend of mine went to have his life insured last week. When he saw me yesterday, he told me what he had learned at the insurance office.
- I work in an insurance office. One day, a man came in and talked with the manager. I overheard their conversation.
- I wanted to buy life insurance for myself. So I went to an insurance office to see the manager.

2　Regroup with students from different groups in step 1. Each student retells the story from his/her previous group.

5　Discuss the following questions in groups of three or four. After the discussion, select one member of your group to report to the class what you have talked about.

1　What do you think of the insurance manager that refuses to sell life insurance to people whose parents died young?

2　Do you think the man should follow the clerk's advice? Why?

3　What would you do if you were the man?

4　Do you think legal actions should be taken against the man and the clerk as well? Why?

Text B

A Difficult Language to Learn

1 Listen to Text B once and answer the following questions.

1 What is the conversation about?

_____

2 Do the three people think it is easy to learn English?

_____

3 Do you think they are native speakers of English?

_____

_____

2 Listen to Text B again. Take notes and answer the questions below.

1 What does "look out" mean?

_____

2 What did Jean think "look out" means?

_____

3 Who do you think shouted "look out"?

_____

4 What did he want to warn people of?

_____

5 What did Yvonne think "All hands on deck" means?

_____

6 What happened when she put her hands on the deck?

_____

7 What did the captain mean when he shouted "All hands on deck"?

_____

8 What time of the day did Michel call on his English friend?

_____

9 Did he see his friend the first time he went to his friend's house? Why?

_____

10 Did he see his friend when he went back half an hour later? Why?

_____

11 What did the maid mean when she said "He's not up yet" and "He's not down yet"?

_____

12 What have you learned about learning English from this conversation?

_____

3 **Describe to your partner the picture below with the following words and expressions.**

three university students
sit on the grass
have a chat
an English textbook
a ridiculous experience
share learning experience
thick blond hair
in a ponytail
a light-colored shirt
dark trousers

4 **Suppose you are an English teacher and your partner plays the role of an English learner. What would you say to him/her when he/she complains that it is difficult to learn a foreign language?**

Text C

They Are Here in My Hand!

1 Read the following text aloud to your partner. Your partner listens to you without looking at the text.

> Mrs. Williams loved flowers and had a small but beautiful garden.
>
> In the summer, her roses were always the best in her street. One summer afternoon, her bell rang, and when she went to the front door, she saw a small boy outside. He was about seven years old, and was holding a big bunch of beautiful roses in his hand.
>
> "I am selling roses," he said. "Do you want any? They are quite cheap. One pound for a big bunch. They are fresh. I picked them this afternoon."
>
> "My boy," Mrs. Williams answered, "I pick roses whenever I want, and don't pay anything for them, because I have lots in my garden."
>
> "Oh, no, you haven't," said the small boy. "There aren't any roses in your garden, because they are here in my hand!"

2 Your partner retells the story to you. Check if any information is missing in his/her retelling.

3 Ask your partner what he/she would do if he/she was Mrs. Williams. You can also share with your partner what you would do if you were Mrs. Williams.

Sentence-making

Pick out useful words and expressions from the following sentences and make sentences with them.

Example

A man **went to** an insurance office **to have his life insured**.

➢ Mary is going to the hairdresser to have her hair cut this weekend.

➢ This morning, Linda went to the tailor's to have her coat lined.

- Father died of tuberculosis at the age of thirty-five.
- We cannot insure your life as your parents were not healthy.
- As the man was leaving the office, he met a clerk.
- The clerk overheard the conversation.
- You must not be so frank and tell the truth.
- No office will insure you if you speak like that.
- Use your imagination a little.
- The man was shown into the office.
- She died from a fall off her bicycle.
- I once heard someone shout "Look out."
- It seems that "look out" may mean "don't look out."
- I put my hands on the deck and someone walked on them.
- I once called early on an English friend.
- Come back in half an hour.
- When I went again for him, she said, "He's not down yet."
- Mrs. Williams loved flowers and had a small but beautiful garden.
- I pick roses whenever I want, and don't pay anything for them.

Scripts

Text A   The Honesty

A man went to an insurance office[1] to have his life insured[2]. The manager of the office asked him how old his parents were when they died.

"Mother had a bad heart[3] and died at the age of thirty. Father died of tuberculosis[4] when he was thirty-five."

"I am very sorry," said the manager. "We cannot insure your life as your parents were not healthy."

As the man was leaving the office, depressed, he met a clerk who had overheard[5] the conversation.

"You must not be so frank[6] and tell the truth," said the clerk, "and no office will insure you if you speak like that. Use your imagination[7] a little."

The man went to another office and was shown into[8] the manager's room.

"Well, young man, how old were your parents when they died?"

"Mother was ninety-three, and she died from a fall off her bicycle. Father was ninety-eight and he died while he was playing football."

Text B   A Difficult Language to Learn

A group of students are talking about their experiences with the English language.

Jean: I once heard someone shout "Look out.[9]" I put my head out of a window and a bucketful of water fell on me[10]. It seems that "look out" may mean "don't look out."[11]

Yvonne: I was once on a ship and heard the captain[12] shout "All hands on deck.[13]" I put my hands on the deck[14] and someone walked on them[15].

Michel: I once called early on an English friend[16] and the maid who came to the door said, "He's not up yet.[17] Come back in half an hour." When I went again for him, she said, "He's not down yet.[18]" I said, "If he's not up and he's not down, where is he?" She said, "He's still in bed. When I say 'He's not up', I mean he has not yet got up, so he has not yet come downstairs."

What do these phrases mean in their respective contexts[19]?

Notes

1 an insurance office: 一家保险公司
2 have his life insured: 让保险公司给他上寿险
3 a bad heart: 心脏不好
4 tuberculosis: 肺结核
5 overheard: 无意中听到
6 so frank: 如此坦率
7 Use your imagination: 发挥你的想象力
8 was shown into: 被领进
9 Look out.: 小心。
10 a bucketful of water fell on me: 一桶水浇到我身上
11 It seems that "look out" may mean "don't look out.": 似乎"look out"的意思是"不要往外看"。
12 the captain: 船长
13 All hands on deck.: 所有人员到甲板上来。
14 I put my hands on the deck: 我把手放到了甲板上
15 someone walked on them: 有人从我手上踩了过去
16 called early on an English friend: 一早去拜访一位英国朋友
17 He's not up yet.: 他还没起床呢。
18 He's not down yet.: 他还没下楼。
19 in their respective contexts: 在它们各自的语境中

Lesson 16

Text A

The Cellphone Rang Again!

1 **Discuss briefly the questions with your partner.**

Have you ever received many phone calls in a short period of time? How did you feel? Do you think cellphone as a life convenience has become a nuisance to private life?

2 **Listen to Text A once and answer the following questions.**

1 What was disturbing Mrs. Moore's evening?

_____

2 Where did the story take place?

_____

3 What time of the day did the story take place?

_____

3 **Listen to Text A again. Take notes and answer the questions below.**

1 Where did Mrs. Moore work?

_____

2 Why did Mrs. Moore look forward to the evening at home?

_____

3 What did she want to do in the evening?

_____

4 Who called when she arrived home?

_____

5 Who were at home with Mrs. Moore? What were they doing?

_____

6 Why did Mrs. Moore go upstairs?

_____

7   Who called when Mrs. Moore reached the top of stairs? Why did he call?

_____

8   What did Mrs. Moore do after she changed clothes?

_____

9   Who called during dinner? Why did they call?

_____

10   Why did Mrs. Moore's neighbor call her?

_____

11   What did Mrs. Moore want to do after cleaning the kitchen?

_____

12   What did Mrs. Moore decide to do for the evening in the end?

_____

13   What did the children feel about her decision?

_____

4 Retell the story of Text A.

1   Form a group of three or four and retell the story together. Take turns to give sentences until the story is completed. You may choose one of the following examples as the beginning of your story.

> - After a day's work, Mrs. Moore wanted to have a good rest in the evening. But she was often disturbed by the cellphone calls.
> - I was always very tired when I got home. All I wanted to do was sit down and do some reading.
> - Mother rarely takes us to watch a movie. But yesterday evening she took us all to the cinema.

2   Regroup with students from different groups in step 1. Each student retells the story from his/her previous group.

5 Discuss the following questions in groups of three or four. After the discussion, select one member of your group to report to the class what you have talked about.

1   Do you think Mrs. Moore was too fussy about her cellphone calls? Why?
2   Do you think it is good to carry a cellphone with you every day? Explain.

Text B

Bill Is Very Rude!

1 **Listen to Text B once and answer the following questions.**

1   Is Bill in his own house?

_____

2   Whose house is it?

_____

2 **Listen to Text B again. Take notes and answer the questions below.**

1   What is Bill doing?

_____

2   Where has Bill put his feet?

_____

3   Is it polite to put his feet there?

_____

4   Why has he put his feet there?

_____

5   Is Victor happy with him? Why?

_____

6   Does Bill put his feet on his own table? Why not?

_____

7   Does Victor want to buy a new table?

_____

8   What does Victor want to do before he buys a new table?

_____

9   How much will Bill pay for the old table? Why?

_____

10   Is Bill a selfish boy? Why?

_____

3 **Describe to your partner the picture below with the following words and expressions.**

a sitting room
a doorknob
a round old table with three legs
a bookcase beside the door
with some books in it
two books on top of the bookcase
a comfortable armchair placed in front of the bookcase
a teenager
sit comfortably in the armchair
lean back
a cushion under his head
sit cross-legged
wear a pair of leather shoes
his feet resting on the table
be badly marked
daydream or watch TV

4 Suppose you are Bill and your partner plays the role of Victor. When you come to visit Victor, you are behaving so rudely that Victor is mad at you. You two talk angrily about good manners of visiting others in their houses.

Text C

Billy's Motorcycle Was Stolen.

1 **Read the following text aloud to your partner. Your partner listens to you without looking at the text.**

Billy's motorcycle shone in the afternoon sun and caught Billy's reflection in the fender. He had worked all summer to save enough money for this bike and it was his—all his. He strapped on his helmet, slid the new black leather gloves over his hands, then threw one leg over the vinyl seat. There was a roar of the engine as he kicked it into motion, and suddenly there he was, speeding down the street on his motorcycle.

Billy's little brother, Tommy, watched solemnly from the front door. Tommy was only eight years old, but eight was old enough, he thought, for someone to have his very own motorcycle. It didn't seem fair that Billy had a bike and Tommy didn't. So Tommy sat on the front porch, ate his candy bar, and brooded over the matter as he watched Billy slide around the corner. All he wanted was just one ride.

When Billy discovered his bike missing the next morning, there was a widespread investigation by the police, his parents, and the neighbors. No one had seen the bike since the day before. As Billy walked off down the sidewalk, heading for the school bus, his attention was attracted by something black glaring at him from under a hedge. He approached slowly, then suddenly broke into a run. There under the hedge was his motorcycle with one badly dented fender.

He reached for the handlebars to pull it from under the bushes. When he retracted his hand, there was a familiar sticky substance on his fingers. Tasting the brown sweetness, Billy smiled secretly to himself. He knew who had taken his motorcycle for a spin.

2 **Your partner retells the story to you. Check if any information is missing in his/her retelling.**

3 **Ask your partner if he/she has lost something and found it again. You can also share with your partner your experience of losing and finding something.**

Sentence-making

Pick out useful words and expressions from the following sentences and make sentences with them.

Example

Would you **mind taking** your feet off the table?

➢ Would you mind taking a photo of me?

➢ Would you mind opening the window?

- She was looking forward to a relaxing evening at home.
- Just as she walked into the room, the cellphone began to ring.
- She smelled dinner cooking and went in to see how her children were getting along with the meal.
- Everything was ready except setting the table.
- She found out that her husband wouldn't be home for dinner.
- During dinner, the cellphone rang twice.
- Her sister called to ask about the family.
- Mrs. Moore sat down with a sigh to read while the children did their homework.
- Will you please avoid marking mine?
- I thought you were going to buy a new table soon.
- I have to sell my old one first.
- Would you please tell me how much you want for it?
- How much do you think it's worth?
- I'll give you ten dollars for it.
- He had worked all summer to save enough money for this bike.
- Eight was old enough, he thought, for someone to have his very own motorcycle.
- He reached for the handlebars to pull it from under the bushes.

Scripts

Text A　The Cellphone Rang Again!

Mrs. Moore had worked hard all day at the office, and she was looking forward to[1] a relaxing evening[2] at home.

Just as[3] she walked into the room, the cellphone began to ring. She answered the phone[4] and found that the caller[5] was a man trying to promote a product. She refused and hung up the phone[6].

She smelled dinner cooking[7] and went in to see how her children were getting along with[8] the meal. Everything was ready except setting the table[9], so Mrs. Moore went upstairs to change clothes[10].

Just as she reached the head of the stairs[11], the cellphone rang again. When Mrs. Moore answered it, she found out that her husband wouldn't be home for dinner[12].

After she changed clothes, she went back downstairs to eat. During dinner, the cellphone rang twice. Her sister called to ask about the family[13], and a volunteer group[14] wanted to invite her to their next meeting[15]. She and the children finished dinner and began cleaning up the kitchen[16]. The cellphone rang again. Her neighbor wanted to borrow the garden hose[17].

After the kitchen was cleaned, Mrs. Moore sat down with a sigh[18] to read while the children did their homework. The cellphone rang again.

Without even answering it[19], Mrs. Moore turned off the cellphone and called to[20] her children, "Get ready[21], we're all going to a movie."

"Great![22]"

Text B　Bill Is Very Rude[23]!

Bill is in Victor's house and he is sitting down. He is leaning back[24] and he has put his feet on the table[25]. Bill is very rude.

Victor: Would you mind[26] taking your feet off the table[27], Bill?
Bill:　　Not at all.[28] But I was very comfortable.
Victor: Do you put your feet on your own table?
Bill:　　No, I never do that.
Victor: Why not?
Bill:　　I don't want to mark my table[29], of course.
Victor: Well, will you please avoid marking mine[30]?
Bill:　　I'm sorry. I thought you were going to buy a new table soon.

Victor: I hope to buy a new table, but I have to sell my old one first.
Bill: Would you please tell me how much you want for it[31]?
Victor: How much do you think it's worth?[32]
Bill: Not much. It's badly marked.[33] I'll give you ten dollars for it.

Notes

1   was looking forward to: 正盼望着

2   a relaxing evening: 一个可以放松的晚上

3   Just as: 就在……的时候

4   answered the phone: 接电话

5   the caller: 打来电话的人

6   hung up the phone: 挂断电话

7   smelled dinner cooking: 闻到做饭的香味

8   were getting along with: ……进展

9   setting the table: 摆桌子

10 change clothes: 换衣服

11 the head of the stairs: 楼梯顶上

12 her husband wouldn't be home for dinner: 她丈夫不回家吃晚饭了

13 ask about the family: 问候全家人

14 a volunteer group: 一个志愿者团体

15 invite her to their next meeting: 邀请她参加下一次会议

16 cleaning up the kitchen: 收拾、打扫厨房

17 the garden hose: 花园里浇水用的软管

18 with a sigh: 叹了一口气

19 Without even answering it: 甚至连电话都不接

20 called to: 对……喊道

21 Get ready: 准备好

22 Great!: 太棒了!

23 Rude: 粗鲁，没有礼貌

24 is leaning back: 向后仰靠

25 has put his feet on the table: 把脚放在桌子上

26 Would you mind: 你是否在意

27 taking your feet off the table: 把你的脚从桌子上拿下来

28 Not at all.: 一点儿也不。

29 mark my table: 在我的桌子上留下痕迹，划坏我的桌子

30 avoid marking mine: 避免划坏我的桌子

31 how much you want for it: 你想把它卖多少钱

32 How much do you think it's worth?: 你觉得它值多少钱?

33 It's badly marked.: 它已被划得很厉害了。

Lesson 17

Text A

The Stolen Smells

1 **Discuss briefly the questions with your partner.**

Do you know the stories of Che Yin who read books by the light of fireflies, Sun Kang who studied hard with the reflection of snow, and Kuang Heng who read by the light through a crack on his wall? Tell these stories to your partner. Do you know any other ancient Chinese stories about studying hard? Share with your partner.

2 **Listen to Text A once and answer the following questions.**

1 What is the story about?

_____

2 How poor was the student?

_____

3 Where did he live?

_____

3 **Listen to Text A again. Take notes and answer the questions below.**

1 Who came to visit the poor student?

_____

2 Was the poor student unhappy about his room?

_____

3 What did his friend think of the food the poor student had?

_____

4 What was the comment on the food that made the restaurant owner angry?

_____

5 Why did the restaurant owner decide to take the student to court?

_____

6 What was the attitude of the people in the court?

_____

7 Did the judge think it was a joke? Explain his attitude.

_____

8 What made the restaurant owner delighted?

_____

9 Why was the poor student afraid?

_____

10 What did the student do when he was asked if he had any money?

_____

11 What was the order from the judge after he saw the coins in the student's hand?

_____

12 What did the people in the court hear?

_____

13 What was the meaning of the order from the judge?

_____

14 Was the restaurant owner well paid for his smells?

_____

4 **Retell the story of Text A.**

1 Form a group of three or four and retell the story together. Take turns to give sentences until the story is completed. You may choose one of the following examples as the beginning of your story.

- A young man came to visit a friend who lived in a room over a restaurant. He found the room very shabby.
- I owned a restaurant. I cooked well and loved money.
- Many years ago, I was a judge. Let me describe to you a very interesting case I handled.
- A long time ago, there was a poor student. He could only afford to rent a tiny shabby room over a restaurant.

2 Regroup with students from different groups in step 1. Each student retells the story from his/her previous group.

5 Discuss the following questions in groups of three or four. After the discussion, select one member of your group to report to the class what you have talked about.

1 Use as many descriptive words as you can to describe the poor student and the restaurant owner.

2 What do you think of the judge? Imagine what kind of person he was.

Text B

What Do the Romans Do?

1 Listen to Text B once and answer the following questions.

1 What are they talking about?

_____

2 Where are they?

_____

3 What do you think they are planning to do?

_____

2 Listen to Text B again. Take notes and answer the questions below.

1 How do the Romans get to work?

_____

2 Do the Romans do what everyone else does?

_____

3 How does the climate in Rome differ from that in England?

_____

4 What does Mrs. Turnbull envy the Romans?

_____

5 What doesn't Mrs. Turnbull like about English weather?

_____

6 What do lots of tourists go to Rome for?

_____

7 Do Mr. and Mrs. Turnbull know how much it costs to fly to Rome?

_____

3 Describe to your partner the picture below with the following words and expressions.

a newly married couple
a sofa in the living room
sit on the sofa
thick blond hair
have short hair
a light-colored shirt
talk with his wife so happily
make their vacation plan
go on their honeymoon

4 Suppose you are Mr. Turnbull and your partner plays the role of his wife. Discuss and make a plan for your holiday in Rome.

Text C

Mrs. Smith Meets Mrs. Turnbull.

1 Play the audio of the following text to your partner. Your partner listens without looking at the text.

Mrs. Smith:	Hello, Mrs. Turnbull. How are you?
Mrs. Turnbull:	Fine, thanks. How's your boy, Jack?
Mrs. Smith:	He's a bit tired. You know, he goes to school at eight o'clock every morning. He doesn't get home till after four. Then he does his homework after tea. It often takes him a couple of hours to finish it.
Mrs. Turnbull:	Poor boy. They work hard at school nowadays, don't they? Does he like it?
Mrs. Smith:	School, you mean? Yes, he does. He likes his teachers, and that always makes a difference.
Mrs. Turnbull:	Yes, it does. Does he go to school by bus?
Mrs. Smith:	No, he walks. He likes walking. He meets some of his friends at the corner and they go together.
Mrs. Turnbull:	What does he do when it rains?
Mrs. Smith:	My husband takes him by car. He passes the school on the way to the office.

2 Your partner retells what the conversation is about. Check if any information is missing in his/her retelling.

3 Ask your partner to tell about a school he/she went to and what he/she liked about it. You can also share your answer with your partner.

Sentence-making

Pick out useful words and expressions from the following sentences and make sentences with them.

Example

It doesn't rain so much **as** it does in England.

➤ I'll behave toward them as I would like to be treated.

- His room was at the back of the building.
- He heard the poor student talking to his friend.
- I am busy with my studies.
- I'm not interested in my room.
- You don't have money for anything tasty.
- The delicious smells make the rice very tasty.
- The mean man accused the student of stealing his smells.
- The judge took him seriously.
- You've been well paid for your smells.
- In other words, the Romans do what everyone else does.
- The climate's different for a start.
- I envy them the sun.
- He knows how to enjoy himself.
- Lots of tourists go to Rome just for the food.
- How much does it cost to fly to Rome?
- He doesn't get home till after four.
- It often takes him a couple of hours to finish it.
- He likes walking.
- He passes the school on the way to the office.

Scripts

Text A   The Stolen Smells

Many years ago in another country, there lived a poor student. He had very little money[1]. He lived in a very small room over a restaurant[2]. His room was at the back of the building over the kitchen[3]. The restaurant owner was a very mean man[4]. Nobody liked him. But he was a good cook and many people came to his restaurant.

One day, he was working quietly in his kitchen when he heard the poor student talking to his friend. "You must be very unhappy," said his friend, "living in a poor room like this[5]."

"Oh no," said the student, "I am busy with my studies[6] and I'm not interested in my room."

"But you only eat plain rice[7]—you don't have money for anything tasty[8]."

"Yes, it's true. I eat only plain rice. But the delicious smells that come from the kitchen make the rice very tasty indeed[9]."

The restaurant owner was furious. This student was stealing the smells from his kitchen. He decided to take him to court[10].

Everybody in the court laughed when the mean man accused the student of stealing his smells[11]. But the judge took him seriously[12]. "Every man should be able to complain to the court[13]," he said.

When the restaurant owner told the judge everything, the judge said, "You are right. The student is guilty.[14]" The restaurant owner was delighted, but the poor student was very much afraid. What could he do? He had only a few coins in his pocket.[15]

The judge asked the student if he had any money. The student took five coins from his pocket and held them out to the judge in his right hand[16].

"Let the coins fall into your left hand," said the judge.

The courtroom was very quiet. Everyone heard the tinkle of the coins as they fell into the student's left hand.[17]

"Well," said the judge to the restaurant owner, "you've heard his money. You've been well paid for your smells.[18]"

Text B   What Do the Romans Do?

Mr. Turnbull: "When in Rome, do as the Romans do[19]," they say.

Mrs. Turnbull: What do the Romans do?

Mr. Turnbull: They live in Rome, of course, and use public transport to get to work. Some people also drive or walk to work.

Mrs. Turnbull: In other words[20], the Romans do what everyone else does.

Mr. Turnbull: Yes, but they do it differently. Everything is different.

Mrs. Turnbull: What do you mean?

Mr. Turnbull: Well, the climate's different for a start[21]. It doesn't rain so much as it does in England. The sun shines more often.

Mrs. Turnbull: I envy them the sun.[22]

Mr. Turnbull: I know. You hate the rain, don't you?

Mrs. Turnbull: I certainly do.

Mr. Turnbull: And a Roman really loves life. He knows how to enjoy himself.[23]

Mrs. Turnbull: They always eat spaghetti[24] and drink wine, don't they?

Mr. Turnbull: Not always. But they like a good meal. Lots of tourists go to Rome just for the food, you know.

Mrs. Turnbull: Really? How much does it cost to fly to Rome?

Mr. Turnbull: I don't know exactly[25], but it costs a lot of money.

Notes

1　had very little money: 几乎没有钱

2　a very small room over a restaurant: 在饭馆上面的一个小房间

3　at the back of the building over the kitchen: 在楼的后面，厨房的上面

4　a very mean man: 一个非常吝啬的人

5　living in a poor room like this: 住在一间这样的破旧屋子里

6　busy with my studies: 忙于学习

7　eat plain rice: 光吃米饭，意思是没有菜

8　you don't have money for anything tasty: 你没钱，吃不起好吃的东西

9　the delicious smells that come from the kitchen make the rice very tasty indeed: 厨房里香气扑鼻的菜味使（我的）米饭变得很好吃

10　take him to court: 把他告上法庭

11　accused the student of stealing his smells: 指控这个学生偷了他的菜香味

12　took him seriously: 很严肃地对待他

13　complain to the court: 向法庭申诉

14　The student is guilty.: 这个学生有罪。

15　He had only a few coins in his pocket.: 他口袋里只有几个硬币。

16　held them out to the judge in his right hand: 伸出拿着硬币的右手让法官看

17　Everyone heard the tinkle of the coins as they fell into the student's left hand.: 每个人都听到了这几个硬币（从右手）落到左手时发出的叮当声。

18　You've been well paid for your smells.: （人家）已给你的菜香味付够钱了。

19　When in Rome, do as the Romans do: 入乡随俗

20　In other words: 换句话说

21   for a start: 首先

22   I envy them the sun.: 我羡慕他们能有阳光。

23   He knows how to enjoy himself.: 他（罗马人）知道如何享受生活。

24   spaghetti: 意大利式面条

25   I don't know exactly: 我不知道具体（要多少钱）

Lesson 18

Text A

How to Make Everybody Happy?

1 **Discuss briefly the questions with your partner.**

Do you try to make people around you happy? Why/Why not?

2 **Listen to Text A once and answer the following questions.**

1 How many people were there in the story?

2 Who were the people in the dialogue? What was their relationship?

3 What were they talking about?

3 **Listen to Text A again. Take notes and answer the questions below.**

1 Where did Peter's uncle live?

2 Where did Peter go once? How long did he stay there?

3 What did they do when Peter was staying with his uncle?

4 What did Peter's uncle do when he took Peter out?

5 Was Peter surprised to see his uncle wave to everybody?

6 What did Peter ask his uncle? Did his uncle know all those people?

7 How did his uncle explain himself?

8   Did Peter understand why his uncle waved to everybody in the end? Why?

_____

4 Retell the story of Text A.

1   Form a group of three or four and retell the story together. Take turns to give sentences until the story is completed. You may choose one of the following examples as the beginning of your story.

> • I have an uncle who lives in the country. One day, I traveled to the country on my own to visit him.
> • Yesterday, my son returned from his trip to the country. He was very excited and told us about his uncle.

2   Regroup with students from different groups in step 1. Each student retells the story from his/her previous group.

5 Discuss the following questions in groups of three or four. After the discussion, select one member of your group to report to the class what you have talked about.

1   Use as many descriptive words as you can to describe Peter's uncle.
2   Do you like Peter's uncle? Explain.

Text B

What Do You Do After Work?

1 Listen to Text B once and answer the following questions.

1   Who are the two people in this dialogue?

_____

2   What is the possible relationship between them?

_____

3   What time of the day do you think it is? Why?

_____

2 **Listen to Text B again. Take notes and answer the questions below.**

1   Where is Jim going?

_____

2   Where is Peter going?

_____

3   Why doesn't Peter go with Jim?

_____

4   How often does Jim go to the cinema?

_____

5   What does Jim usually do in the evening?

_____

6   Does Jim know what is on TV that night?

_____

7   Where is Jim's wife going for the holiday?

_____

8   How long is she going to stay there?

_____

9   Where does Jim's mother-in-law live?

_____

10   Where does Jim want to go for his holiday this year?

_____

11   Does Jim like to spend his holiday by the sea?

_____

12   Why isn't Jim going with his wife?

_____

13   What's Peter going to do for his holiday?

_____

14   Why isn't Peter going abroad?

_____

3 **Describe to your partner the picture below with the following words and expressions.**

a clock on the wall

between the two windows

two men in suits

wear a tie

with a briefcase in his right hand

with a folder under his right arm

wear glasses

get off work

get out of the office

have a chat

with his left hand in his pocket

4 **Suppose you are Peter and your partner plays the role of Jim. Talk about your favorite TV program or movie.**

Text C

Going to the Theater

1 Read the following text aloud to your partner. Your partner listens to you without looking at the text.

> If you want to be certain of seeing a play in London, you have to book your seat in advance. You can buy your tickets either online or at the box office in the theater itself. It is very rare that you will be lucky enough to get a ticket five minutes before the play begins. If you go in a big group, it is not always possible for all of you to sit in the same part of the theater. Some will have to sit in the stalls, others in the dress circle and some in the upper circle.

2 Your partner retells the story to you. Check if any information is missing in his/her retelling.

3 Ask your partner if he/she has bought theater tickets before. If yes, ask him/her to share the experience. You could also share yours. Introduce the context first, and then tell your story.

Sentence-making

Pick out useful words and expressions from the following sentences and make sentences with them.

Example

Where did you meet **them all**?

➤ Mom said that dad would take us all to the park tomorrow.
➤ Henry is still doing his assignments. He can't watch TV until he has finished them all.

- Peter went to stay with him for a few weeks.
- Whenever they went for a walk and they passed somebody, his uncle waved.
- He continues his journey with a happier heart.
- So he has something to think about during the rest of his journey, and that makes his journey seem shorter.
- What about coming with me?
- I believe it's a very good film.
- Do you go to the cinema a lot?
- Do you know what's on the telly tonight, by any chance?
- My wife's going to her mother's for a couple of weeks.
- I need peace and quietness when I'm on holiday.
- It's going to take every penny I've got.
- If you want to be certain of seeing a play in London, you have to book your seat in advance.
- It is very rare that you will be lucky enough to get a ticket five minutes before the play begins.

Scripts

Text A   How to Make Everybody Happy?

Peter's uncle lived in the country[1]. Once Peter went to stay with him for a few weeks[2]. Whenever they went for a walk or for a drive in the car[3] and they passed somebody, his uncle waved. Peter was surprised, and said, "Uncle George, you know everybody here. Where did you meet them all?" "I don't know all these people," said his uncle. "Then why do you wave to them?" asked Peter.

"Well, Peter," answered his uncle, "when I wave to someone and he knows me, he is pleased[4]. He continues his journey with a happier heart[5]. But when I wave to someone and he doesn't know me, he is surprised and says to himself, 'Who is that man? Why did he wave to me?' So he has something to think about during the rest of his journey, and that makes his journey seem shorter. So I make everybody happy."

Text B What Do You Do After Work?

Peter: Hello, Jim. Where are you going?

Jim:　Hello, Peter. To the cinema. What about coming with me?[6]

Peter: No, thanks. I'm going home. My wife's expecting me.[7]

Jim:　What a pity.[8] I believe it's a very good film.

Peter: Do you go to the cinema a lot?[9]

Jim:　Once a week.[10] Most nights I sit at home and watch telly[11].

Peter: Do you know what's on the telly tonight[12], by any chance[13]?

Jim:　No, I'm sorry, I don't.

Peter: Oh, I see. By the way, where are you going for your holiday[14] this year?

Jim:　I don't know yet. My wife's going to her mother's for a couple of weeks[15]. She lives by the sea[16], you know.

Peter: Oh, does she? That's convenient[17].

Jim:　Yes, but I want to go to the country[18].

Peter: Don't you like the sea?

Jim:　Yes, very much. But I need peace and quietness when I'm on holiday[19]. What are you going to do?

Peter: I'm going to stay at home.

Jim:　Aren't you going to have a holiday abroad this year?

Peter: No, I want to buy a car, and that's going to take every penny I've got[20].

Notes

1　in the country: 在乡村

2　stay with him for a few weeks: 和他小住几个星期

3　for a drive in the car: 开车去兜风

4　he is pleased: 他感到高兴

5　with a happier heart: 心情更为愉悦

6　What about coming with me?: 同我一起去怎么样？

7　My wife's expecting me.: 我的妻子在等我。

8　What a pity.: 真遗憾。

9　Do you go to the cinema a lot?: 你经常去看电影吗？

10　Once a week.: 一周一次。

11　telly (television): 电视

12　what's on the telly tonight: 今天晚上有什么电视节目

13　by any chance: 碰巧

14　where are you going for your holiday: 你打算去哪儿度假

15　a couple of weeks: 一两个星期

16　by the sea: 在海边

17　convenient: 方便的

18　go to the country: 去乡下

19　I need peace and quietness when I'm on holiday: 度假时我需要祥和安静的环境

20　take every penny I've got: 花掉我所有的钱，把我挣的钱花得一分都不剩

Lesson 19

Text A

A One-hundred-dollar Bill

1 **Discuss briefly the questions with your partner.**

Have you ever picked up things other people lost? What did you do with it?

2 **Listen to Text A once and answer the following questions.**

1 Where did the story take place?

_____

2 What is the story about?

_____

3 How do you know he was a schoolboy?

_____

3 **Listen to Text A again. Take notes and answer the questions below.**

1 There weren't many people at the grocery store, were there?

_____

2 What was Sam doing at the grocery store?

_____

3 Did he often do the chores at home?

_____

4 Did he enjoy doing them?

_____

5 What was he thinking of while waiting in the long line?

_____

6 Why did he want to buy a camera?

_____

7 Did he have enough money to buy the camera?

_____

8 How much more money did he need to buy the camera?

_____

9 How could he get the money he needed and how long would it take?

_____

10 What happened to him while he was waiting?

_____

11 Who was it that shoved him aside?

_____

12 Where did she live?

_____

13 What kind of person was she?

_____

14 Was she in a hurry? How do you know?

_____

15 What did Sam notice?

_____

16 What did Sam do then?

_____

17 What was Sam thinking as he bent to pick up the money?

_____

4 Retell the story of Text A.

1 Form a group of three or four and retell the story together. Take turns to give sentences until the story is completed. You may choose one of the following examples as the beginning of your story.

- My son, Sam, has always been eager to help out with house chores. He often helps me do shopping and other things.
- As a schoolboy, I was already a good helping hand to my parents. I especially enjoyed shopping for my mother.
- I went shopping the other day. But the cashier was very slow and it took the cashier a long time to give me my change. I was very unhappy.

2 Regroup with students from different groups in step 1. Each student retells the story from his/her previous group.

5 Discuss the following questions in groups of three or four. After the discussion, select one member of your group to report to the class what you have talked about.

1   Say as much as you can to describe Sam and Mrs. Sanders.
2   Sam is right to return the money to Mrs. Sanders in spite of her bad behavior. Talk with your group members what you would say to Mrs. Sanders if you were Sam.

Text B

A Babysitter

1 **Listen to Text B once and answer the following questions.**

1   Who took part in the conversation?

_____

2   What did they talk about?

_____

3   Where was Colin the night before?

_____

2 **Listen to Text B again. Take notes and answer the questions below.**

1   Why did Colin's parents make him stay at home?

_____

2   Did Colin mind looking after his baby brother?

_____

3   Why didn't Colin mind babysitting at home?

_____

4   What else did Colin do?

_____

5   How long did Colin watch the boxing?

_____

6   Did Jack like to watch the boxing on TV?

_____

7   Why didn't Jack watch it that night?

_____

8   Would Jack enjoy looking after his baby brother at home if he had one?

_____

9   How can you tell?

_____

3 Describe to your partner the picture below with the following words and expressions.

a newborn baby
a baby of about one year old
a babysitter
a teenager/schoolboy
look after the baby
a baby's cot
a soft pillow
a warm quilt
fall asleep
sleep on his back/side
time for sports program on Channel X
turn on TV
the remote control
sit on a cushion on the floor
a program
a live broadcasting of a boxing match
play with his baby brother for a while
bottle-feed the baby for the last time of the day
cannot be happier
have a happy and rewarding evening

4 Suppose you are Colin and your partner is Jack. Both of you want very much to watch your favorite singer's performance, but do not agree on whether to watch the live broadcast or to go to the concert. Try to convince each other.

Text C

Miss Green Goes On a Diet.

1 Read the following text aloud to your partner. Your partner listens to you without looking at the text.

Miss Green was very fat. She weighed 100 kilos, and she was getting heavier every month, so she went to see her doctor.

The doctor said, "You need a diet, Miss Green, and I've got a good one here." He gave her a small book and said, "Read this carefully and eat the things on page 11 every day. Then come back and see me in two weeks' time."

Miss Green came again two weeks later, but she wasn't thinner: She was fatter. The doctor was surprised and said, "Are you eating the things on page 11 of the small book?"

"Yes, Doctor," she answered.

The next day the doctor visited Miss Green during her dinner. She was very surprised to see him.

"Miss Green," he said, "Why are you eating potatoes and bread? They aren't in your diet."

"But, Doctor," Miss Green answered, "I ate my diet at lunch time. This is my dinner."

2 Your partner retells the story to you. Check if any information is missing in his/her retelling.

3 Ask your partner what he/she thinks is the best way to keep fit. Invite him/her to share some successful ways. You can also share yours.

Sentence-making

Pick out useful words and expressions from the following sentences and make sentences with them.

Example

Jack went out, **but** Colin **had to** stay at home.

➤ Bill went out to swim with his friends, but his sister had to stay at home and cook dinner.

➤ Tim likes bread, but he had to eat rice when he was on a business trip last week.

- Sam waited patiently in the long line at the grocery store.
- He enjoyed helping out at home.
- He daydreamed about the new camera he wanted to buy.
- He wanted to buy it soon because his family was going on a vacation.
- He wanted to take pictures during their trip.
- He needed seventy more dollars to buy the camera.
- His lawn-mowing job at the Smith's should provide the money shortly.
- She had shoved in front of him without even smiling.
- Mrs. Sanders was too busy criticizing the cashier for his slowness to notice.
- As Sam bent to pick up the money, he thought quickly.
- They wanted to go out, so they made me look after my baby brother.
- Didn't you mind doing it?
- My brother was very good and I did quite a lot of homework.
- What was on television last night?
- What a pity I missed it last night!
- She weighed 100 kilos, and she was getting heavier every month.
- She was very surprised to see him.
- I ate my diet at lunch time.

Scripts

Text A   A One-hundred-dollar Bill[1]

Sam waited patiently in the long line[2] at the grocery store[3]. He had come to pick up a few items for his mother[4]. He often did the chores[5] for his parents after school. He enjoyed helping out at home[6]. As he waited, he daydreamed[7] about the new camera he wanted to buy. He wanted to buy it soon because his family was going on a vacation[8], and he wanted to take pictures during their trip. There was only one problem. He needed seventy more dollars to buy the camera. His lawn-mowing job at the Smith's should provide the money shortly.[9]

Suddenly Sam was roughly shoved aside[10]. He recognized Mrs. Sanders, an unkind and unfriendly woman who lived in his block[11]. She had shoved in front of him without even smiling. Just as Mrs. Sanders received her change and her purchases[12], a one-hundred-dollar bill flew out of her hand and fell at Sam's feet. Mrs. Sanders, however, was too busy criticizing the cashier for his slowness[13] to notice. As Sam bent to pick up the money, he thought quickly[14]. The money did belong to Mrs. Sanders[15], but it dropped on the floor, and, with it, he could buy the camera. But, on second thought, buying the camera with the money was not a good idea and his part-time wage would be paid soon. After thinking for a while, he returned the money to Mrs. Sanders.

Text B   A Babysitter

Colin is talking to Jack about what he did the night before. Jack went out, but Colin had to stay at home.

Jack: Why did your parents make you stay at home[16]?
Colin: They wanted to go out, so they made me look after my baby brother.
Jack: Didn't you mind doing it?[17]
Colin: No, I didn't. My brother was very good[18] and I did quite a lot of homework.
Jack: Didn't you even[19] want to go to the cinema?
Colin: Not really.[20] I watched television for an hour.
Jack: What was on television last night?
Colin: Boxing. It was excellent.
Jack: Oh. I enjoy watching boxing on television, too. What a pity I missed it last night!

Colin: What did you do last night?

Jack: I went to a football match in the sports stadium[21].

Notes

1   A One-hundred-dollar Bill: 一张 100 美元的钞票
2   waited patiently in the long line: 耐心地排在长队里
3   at the grocery store: 在食品杂货店里
4   pick up a few items for his mother: 帮他妈妈买几样东西
5   did the chores: 做家务
6   helping out at home: 在家里帮忙
7   daydreamed: 幻想
8   was going on a vacation: 要去度假
9   His lawn-mowing job at the Smith's should provide the money shortly.: 用不了多久，他在史密斯家割草坪所挣的钱就可以补上所缺的钱了。
10   was roughly shoved aside: 被猛推到一边
11   lived in his block: 与他住在同一街区
12   received her change and her purchases: 拿起找给她的钱和她采购的物品
13   criticizing the cashier for his slowness: 批评收银员动作太慢
14   he thought quickly: 他的脑子很快地转动起来
15   The money did belong to Mrs. Sanders: 这钱确实属于桑德斯夫人
16   make you stay at home: 让你待在家里
17   Didn't you mind doing it?: 难道你不介意那样做吗?
18   My brother was very good: 我弟弟很乖、很听话
19   even: 甚至，加重语气词
20   Not really.: 不太想。
21   the sports stadium: 体育场

Lesson 20

Text A

What Are the Times of Meals?

1 **Discuss briefly the questions with your partner.**

Have you ever stayed in a hotel? Share your journey with your partner.

2 **Listen to Text A once and answer the following questions.**

1 What is the story about?

_____

2 What time of the year was it?

_____

3 Did Mr. and Mrs. Williams often stay in a good hotel when they were on holiday?

_____

3 **Listen to Text A again. Take notes and answer the questions below.**

1 Where did Mr. and Mrs. Williams always spend their summer holidays?

_____

2 Why did they decide to go to Rome one year?

_____

3 Where did they plan to stay?

_____

4 What did they want to do in the city?

_____

5 How did they go to Rome?

_____

6 When did they arrive at their hotel?

_____

7   Did they expect that dinner would be served late in the evening? Why not?

_____

8   Why were they surprised?

_____

9   What were the times of meals?

_____

10   Why was Mrs. Williams disappointed?

_____

11   Do you think they would have time to see the sights of Rome? Explain.

_____

4 Retell the story of Text A.

1   Form a group of three or four and retell the story together. Take turns to give sentences until the story is completed. You may choose one of the following examples as the beginning of your story.

- Mr. and Mrs. Williams had never been to any places outside England. Neither had they ever stayed in a good hotel.
- Mr. and Mrs. Williams arrived at a good hotel in Rome late one evening. They were surprised to find that dinner was still being served.
- One year, Mr. Williams made a lot of money in his business. So he and his wife decided to spend their summer holidays in Rome.

2   Regroup with students from different groups in step 1. Each student retells the story from his/her previous group.

5 Discuss the following questions in groups of three or four. After the discussion, select one member of your group to report to the class what you have talked about.

1   Use as many descriptive words as you can to describe Mr. and Mrs. Williams.
2   Do you think Mr. and Mrs. Williams would enjoy themselves in the hotel? Why/Why not?
3   What are the things you would consider when booking accommodation for short trips?

Text B

The Food Is Bad.

1 **Listen to Text B once and answer the following questions.**

1　Were Lise, Nick and Bill staying in a good hotel?

_____

2　What do you think was their relationship?

_____

3　What age group did they belong to?

_____

2 **Listen to Text B again. Take notes and answer the questions below.**

1　What had Lise, Nick and Bill done?

_____

2　When did Nick get back?

_____

3　When did Bill and Lise get back?

_____

4　What were the others in the youth hostel doing when they came back?

_____

5　Why did they go and get their food immediately after they came back?

_____

6　Did they like the food in the youth hostel? Why not?

_____

7　Did they like the warden? Why not?

_____

8　What did they decide to do?

_____

3 **Describe to your partner the picture below with the following words and expressions.**

a young man in his early twenties

wear short hair

be dressed in

a strong person

in a dark-colored T-shirt

hold a fork in his right hand and a knife in his left hand

a left hander (perhaps)

fair-haired

cut a piece of meat

a plate with some roast potatoes and meat in it

a cup of coffee

several slices of toast

two cruets

a small/big meal

complain about the (poor) quality of the food

the meat is too tough

be fed up with

doesn't look very happy

4 **Suppose you are Steve and your partner plays the role of Lise. You are talking about the poor service of the youth hostel and agree to write a letter of complaint to the secretary of the Youth Hostel Association. Discuss what to put in the letter.**

Text C

What Would You Like to Do Tonight?

1 **Play the audio of the following text to your partner. Your partner listens without looking at the text.**

> Mary's cousins, Fay and Rosemary, are still at her house. The girls want to go to the movies. They check on the Internet to see what time the movie starts.
>
> After seeing the movie, they go to an ice cream parlor and order their favorite desserts.
>
> Mary: Girls, what would you like to do tonight?
> Rosemary: Do you want to go to the movies?
> Mary: Of course. I like watching movies.
> Rosemary: Well, let's go to the movies.
> Mary: There's a good movie: *Mulan*.
> Fay: Fine. I heard it's a very good movie.
> Rosemary: Let's find out what time it starts.
> Fay: Here it is. *Mulan* starts at 8 o'clock.

2 **Your partner retells what the conversation is about. Check if any information is missing in his/her retelling.**

3 **Share with your partner your favorite Chinese movie or TV series and explain the reason.**

Sentence-making

Pick out useful words and expressions from the following sentences and make sentences with them.

Example

They **decided to go** to Rome.

➤ We have decided to go to the Summer Palace.
➤ They have decided to go on a picnic if the weather permits.

- They arrived at their hotel late one evening.
- They expected that they would have to go to bed hungry.
- We serve it until half past nine.
- But that hardly leaves any time for us to see the sights of Rome!
- Mrs. Williams said in a disappointed voice.
- It was half past seven when Bill and Lise came in.
- Are hostels in England always as bad as this?
- I haven't stayed in one for ages.
- They check on the Internet to see what time the movie starts.
- Let's find out what time it starts.

Scripts

Text A   What Are the Times of Meals?

Mr. and Mrs. Williams always spent their summer holidays in England in the past, in a small boarding house[1] at the seaside. One year, however, Mr. Williams made a lot of money in his business[2], so they decided to go to Rome and stay in a really good hotel while they went around and saw the sights of that famous city[3].

They flew to Rome, and arrived at their hotel late one evening. They expected that they would have to go to bed hungry[4], because in the boarding houses they had been to in the past, no meals were served after seven o'clock in the evening[5]. They were therefore surprised when the clerk who received them in the hall of the hotel asked them whether they would be taking dinner there[6] that night.

"Are you still serving dinner then?" asked Mrs. Williams.

"Yes, certainly, Madam," answered the clerk. "We serve it until half past nine."

"What are the times of meals then?[7]" asked Mr. Williams.

"Well, sir," answered the clerk, "we serve breakfast from seven to half past eleven in the morning, lunch from twelve to three in the afternoon, tea from four to five[8], and dinner from six to half past nine."

"But that hardly leaves any time for us to see the sights of Rome[9]!" said Mrs. Williams in a disappointed voice[10].

Text B　The Food Is Bad.

Lise, Nick and Bill had gone out walking for the day[11]. Nick got back about six. "Haven't Bill and Lise arrived yet?" he asked. "I thought they were ahead of me[12]..."

It was half past seven when Bill and Lise came in. The others were just finishing supper. "Where on earth have you been?" Nick asked.

"We'll tell you all about it after supper," Bill said. "We'd better go and get our food. The warden's[13] already told us that we're late..."

After supper, the group sat around talking[14].

Steve:　Ugh! The food here is really bad. My soup was cold. And the meat—Huh!— was like leather!

Lise:　Yes, and they don't give you very much, either. I'm still hungry. Are hostels[15] in England always as bad as this?

Anna:　I haven't stayed in one for ages[16]. But I'm sure this one is especially bad. And the warden is so unpleasant...

Malc:　"Don't do this; don't do that. You mustn't do this; you can't do that..."

Steve:　Well, I'm going to write a letter of complaint[17] to the secretary of the Youth Hostel Association!

Lise:　And we'll help you...

Notes

1　a small boarding house: 一个小的寄宿公寓

2　made a lot of money in his business: 做生意挣了许多钱

3　went around and saw the sights of that famous city: 四处游览，观看那座著名城市的风光

4　go to bed hungry: 饿着肚子去睡觉

5　no meals were served after seven o'clock in the evening: 晚上 7 点以后不供应饭食

6   whether they would be taking dinner there: 他们是否要在那里用餐

7   What are the times of meals then?: 那么哪些是用餐时间?

8   tea from four to five: 4 点到 5 点供应午后茶点

9   that hardly leaves any time for us to see the sights of Rome: 这几乎没有给我们空出什么时间来观赏罗马风光

10   in a disappointed voice: 说话的声音显出失望

11   had gone out walking for the day: 白天外出散步

12   they were ahead of me: 他们在我前面

13   The warden: 管理员

14   sat around talking: 围坐在一起聊天

15   hostels:（廉价的）旅社

16   for ages: 好久，很长一段时间

17   a letter of complaint: 一封投诉信

Lesson 21

Text A

Under a Terrible Strain

1 **Discuss briefly the questions with your partner.**

Do you often feel you are under a terrible strain in your daily life? How do you deal with it? Try to give some advice.

2 **Listen to Text A once and answer the following questions.**

1 What is the conversation about?

_____

2 What does Betty say about sleeping pills?

_____

3 Did Betty take her doctor's advice or not?

_____

3 **Listen to Text A again. Take notes and answer the questions below.**

1 Where are Betty and Jean?

_____

2 What is it that Betty wants to know?

_____

3 What does Jean tell Betty about the party the night before?

_____

4 What does Jean ask Betty?

_____

5 What does Betty say in reply?

_____

6 Why couldn't Betty sleep well the night before?

_____

7   What does Jean suggest Betty should have done?

_____

8   How many sleeping pills did Betty use to take every night?

_____

9   Why did Betty have to take so many sleeping pills?

_____

10 How did Betty feel the next morning?

_____

11 What did Betty's doctor say to her?

_____

4 **Retell the story of Text A.**

1   Form a group of three or four and retell the story together. Take turns to give sentences until the story is completed. You may choose one of the following examples as the beginning of your story.

> • Last night, I was swamped with work and couldn't go to the party that my friends had planned for weeks. I felt terrible but had to prioritize my job.
> • I have a friend named Betty who didn't attend the party yesterday because of work. On our way to work today, she confided in me that she suffered from insomnia.

2   Regroup with students from different groups in step 1. Each student retells the story from his/her previous group.

5 **Discuss the following questions in groups of three or four. After the discussion, select one member of your group to report to the class what you have talked about.**

1   What was the trouble with Betty?
2   Do you agree with the saying "All work and no play makes Jack a dull boy"? Give your reasons.

Text B

The Shopping List

1 **Listen to Text B once and answer the following questions.**

1　What was the trouble with Mrs. Black?

_____

2　Who gave Mrs. Black a list of things she shouldn't eat?

_____

3　What did she do about it?

_____

2 **Listen to Text B again. Take notes and answer the questions below.**

1　Where did the doctor send Mrs. Black?

_____

2　What was Mrs. Black given there?

_____

3　What did the hospital do with the results of the tests?

_____

4　What did her doctor do the next morning?

_____

5　What did Mrs. Black do as she listened to her doctor speaking on the phone?

_____

6　What did she do after she had hung up?

_____

7　When did she come back home?

_____

8　What did she find upon her return?

_____

9　What had her husband done for her?

_____

10　Was Mrs. Black happy or not while her husband was trying to be helpful at home?

_____

3 **Describe to your partner the picture below with the following words and expressions.**

in the hall of a well-furnished house
a painting on the wall
a big looking glass
a middle-aged man
look a bit bald
a man with a big nose
be dressed formally
have a list in his hand
look puzzled
seem to have done some shopping
a basket full of things/packages
a basket beside the man in the hall
a middle-aged woman
be dressed in a coat
with a dark-colored handbag
return home from...
stand by the door
notice the basket
be greatly surprised
point to the basket
some misunderstanding between the man and the woman

4 Suppose you are Mrs. Black and your partner plays the role of Mr. Black. Talk about your trouble with your skin and what your doctor has told you. Ask your husband what caused the misunderstanding.

Text C

A Language Mix-up

1 Read the following text aloud to your partner. Your partner listens to you without looking at the text.

> Two young British tourists were traveling in France when a policeman stopped their car and gave it a search. He found a bag of white powder which looked suspicious. "Drogue?" asked the heroin-conscious policeman. "Yes, dogs," they responded, and promptly found themselves in jail. Analysis of the powder revealed that it was a chemical which gave off a smell, used to discourage dogs from using the sides of the car as a toilet. The tourists were set free, after promising to take a few French lessons before their next vacation in France.

2 Your partner retells the story to you. Check if any information is missing in his/her retelling.

3 Tell your partner a story about the misunderstanding caused by the differences in pronunciation. It can be something you heard about or you personally experienced.

Sentence-making

Pick out useful words and expressions from the following sentences and make sentences with them.

Example

The hospital sent the results of the tests **directly** to Mrs. Black's doctor.

➤ After I walked out of the theater, I went home directly.

- What was the party like last night, Jean?
- There were one or two interesting people there.
- I couldn't get away from work early.
- I stopped drinking coffee late at night.
- He could not find anything wrong with her, however.
- It might be the cause of her skin trouble.
- Mrs. Black carefully wrote all the things down on a piece of paper, which she then left on the table.
- When she got back home two hours later, she found her husband waiting for her.
- She asked in surprise.
- When I got home, I found your shopping list on the table.
- They found themselves in jail.
- It was a chemical used to discourage dogs from using the sides of the car as a toilet.
- The tourists were set free.

Scripts

Text A   Under a Terrible Strain[1]

Betty and Jean are on their way to work.

Betty: What was the party like last night[2], Jean?

Jean: Not bad at all, thanks. There were one or two interesting people there. Why couldn't you come?

Betty: Well, I couldn't get away from work early. And when I got home, I had a headache, so I had to go straight to bed. But I wasn't able to get to sleep for hours, because I was overtired.

Jean: What a shame.[3] Why didn't you take a sleeping pill[4]?

Betty: I don't like them. I used to take them[5] when I had to work overtime[6], you know.

Jean: How many did you use to take?

Betty: Three every night.

Jean: Good heavens![7] Why did you take so many?

Betty: Because I was under a terrible strain. The doctor said they weren't very strong. Anyway, I used to feel awful the next morning.[8]

Jean: I'm sure you did.

Betty: The doctor said I had to be careful.

Jean: He was quite right.

Betty: So I stopped taking sleeping pills and drinking coffee late at night.

Text B   The Shopping List

Mrs. Black was having a lot of trouble with her skin[9], so she went to her doctor about it[10]. He could not find anything wrong with her, however, so he sent her to the local hospital for tests[11]. The hospital, of course, sent the results of the tests directly to Mrs. Black's doctor[12]. And the next morning, he phoned her to give her a list of the things that he thought she should not eat, as any of them might be the cause of her skin trouble[13].

Mrs. Black carefully wrote all the things down on a piece of paper, which she then left on the table while she went out to a ladies' meeting.

When she got back home two hours later, she found her husband waiting for her.

He had a big basket full of packages[14] beside him, and when he saw her, he said,

"Hullo, dear. I have done all your shopping for you."

"Done all my shopping?" she asked in surprise. "But how did you know what I wanted?"

"Well, when I got home, I found your shopping list on the table," answered her husband, "so I went down to the shops and bought everything you had written down."

Of course, Mrs. Black had to tell him that he had bought all the things the doctor did not allow her to eat!

Notes

1   Under a Terrible Strain: 过度疲劳，极度紧张
2   What was the party like last night: 昨晚的派对如何
3   What a shame.: 真糟糕。
4   take a sleeping pill: 服用一粒安眠药
5   used to take them: 过去常常服用（安眠药）
6   work overtime: 工作加班加点
7   Good heavens!: 天啊！
8   Anyway, I used to feel awful the next morning.: 总之，我过去常常在第二天早晨感到不适。
9   having a lot of trouble with her skin: 皮肤总出毛病
10 went to her doctor about it: 去她的医生那里看病
11 sent her to the local hospital for tests: 让她去当地的医院做些化验检查
12 sent the results of the tests directly to Mrs. Black's doctor: 把化验结果直接寄给了布莱克夫人的医生
13 might be the cause of her skin trouble: 可能是引起她的皮肤病的原因
14 a big basket full of packages: 装满大包小包的一个大篮子

Lesson 22

Text A

Some Sausage Sandwiches

1 **Discuss briefly the questions with your partner.**

Do you have a plan to keep a pet? Why/Why not?

2 **Listen to Text A once and answer the following questions.**

1 What is the story about?

_____

2 How many people are there in the story? Who are they?

_____

3 What is their relationship?

_____

3 **Listen to Text A again. Take notes and answer the questions below.**

1 When did the story take place?

_____

2 What did Mrs. Andrews do one morning?

_____

3 What did Mrs. Andrews do with the sausage left over?

_____

4 What was wrong with the dog that morning?

_____

5 What did Mrs. Andrews think when she found the dog ill?

_____

6 What did Mrs. Andrews suddenly remember?

_____

7 What did Mrs. Andrews do then?

_____

8   What did Mrs. Andrews tell Mr. Andrews on the phone?

_____

9   When did Jim come home?

_____

10   What did Jim tell his wife when he came back?

_____

11   How were Jim and Henry the next morning?

_____

12   Who came at nine o'clock?

_____

13   What did the milkman ask Mrs. Andrews?

_____

14   Why had the milkman been thinking about Henry?

_____

4   **Retell the story of Text A.**

1   Form a group of three or four and retell the story together. Take turns to give sentences until the story is completed. You may choose one of the following examples as the beginning of your story.

- One morning last summer, my dog, Henry, suddenly got ill. I was very worried.
- Medicine is used to help people recover from their illnesses. But I once took some medicine which made me very sick.
- Yesterday morning, I went to Mrs. Andrews' at the usual time to deliver the milk. I was about to leave the bottles in the milk box outside the gate when suddenly a dog rushed out from the yard.

2   Regroup with students from different groups in step 1. Each student retells the story from his/her previous group.

5   **Discuss the following questions in groups of three or four. After the discussion, select one member of your group to report to the class what you have talked about.**

1   Was there a lesson for Mrs. Andrews to learn? What was it?
2   Would you blame the milkman if you were Mrs. Andrews? Why/Why not?

Text B

Which of the Two Is Better?

1 **Listen to Text B once and answer the following questions.**

1   Where does this dialogue take place?

2   How many people are there? Who are they?

3   What are they talking about?

2 **Listen to Text B again. Take notes and answer the questions below.**

1   What does the woman want to buy?

2   What does the woman ask the salesman?

3   What does the salesman tell her?

4   What does the salesman say about the expensive computer?

5   What does the woman want the computer for?

6   What does the salesman say about the cheaper computer then?

7   Which computer does the woman buy finally?

8   How does the woman want to pay for the computer?

9   Does the store accept cash?

3 **Describe to your partner the picture below with the following words and expressions.**

a shop selling electrical goods
a department store
a department of electrical appliances
a shop assistant
difficult to tell his age
in his 30's or 40's
a clean-shaven face
a tie in stripes
computers of various brands
screens of various sizes
big ones for home use
portable ones
a lady with a handbag
a customer
point at
consult

4 **Suppose you are the customer in the shop and your partner plays the role of the salesman. What do you want to know when you buy computers? Make a conversation with your partner.**

Text C

I'll Have One Handy.

1 Read the following text aloud to your partner. Your partner listens to you without looking at the text.

> One rainy evening, my husband, John, and I emerged from a restaurant only to find that he had locked the keys in the car. He insisted he could open the door with a wire coat hanger, so we went back to the restaurant to get one. There was none to be found.
>
> John then ran to a department store a quarter-mile away and returned with a hanger. After a few attempts, he opened the door and we got in. As we sat there, soaked and cold, he stuck the hanger under his seat.
>
> With a smug grin, he said, "Now if this ever happens again, I'll have one handy."

2 Your partner retells the story to you. Check if any information is missing in his/her retelling.

3 Tell your partner about the prevention measures you took after you recovered what had been lost, for instance, your student ID card, the key to your dormitory, or your cellphone and how effective those measures proved to be.

Sentence-making

Pick out useful words and expressions from the following sentences and make sentences with them.

Example

There was one sausage **left over**.

> ➢ I had the rice left over from yesterday.
> ➢ We finished everything and there was nothing left over at all.

- One morning, Mrs. Andrews made some sausage sandwiches for her husband.
- She didn't care for sausages herself.
- He wouldn't stop shaking his head.
- He couldn't stand up properly.
- He has eaten something that didn't agree with him.
- I hope you haven't eaten any of those sandwiches yet.
- I had a very unpleasant hour with the doctor.
- The medicine made me very sick.
- He seems alright now.
- Which of the two computers do you think is better?
- I mean, what's the difference between them?
- This one costs more.
- This part of it is made of high-quality plastic.
- I only want the computer for watching movies.
- I like to watch movies when I get home from work.
- The other computer is good for the money.
- All our customers are satisfied with them.
- John and I emerged from a restaurant only to find that...
- We sat there, soaked and cold.

Scripts

Text A   Some Sausage Sandwiches[1]

One morning last summer, Mrs. Andrews made some sausage sandwiches for her husband's lunch. There was one sausage left over.[2] Mrs. Andrews didn't care for[3] sausages herself, so she gave the last one to Henry, their little dog. Henry ate it up quickly.

During the morning, the dog got ill. He wouldn't stop shaking his head[4] and he couldn't stand up properly[5]. Mrs. Andrews thought, "He has eaten something that didn't agree with him[6]. Maybe that sausage was bad..." She suddenly remembered[7] her husband's lunch. She hurriedly called her husband, Jim, at the office.

"Jim, I hope you haven't eaten any of those sandwiches yet."

"Yes, I have..."

"You have?[8] Well, listen, don't eat any more. I gave Henry the last sausage and now he's ill. Go to the doctor, Jim. Tell the doctor about the dog.[9] Get some medicine at once."

Jim came home at lunchtime and went to bed. "I had a very unpleasant hour with the doctor[10]," he told his wife. "The medicine made me very sick.[11]"

The next morning, Jim was fine. Henry seemed quite well again[12] too. At nine o'clock, the milkman came with the milk[13].

"Good morning, Mrs. Andrews," the milkman said. "How's your dog this morning? I have been thinking about him..."

"Have you?[14] Well, he seems alright now, but..."

"Yesterday morning, he and I had a little accident[15]. He jumped up at me and I dropped a bottle of milk on his head."

Text B   Which of the Two Is Better?

Woman: Which of the two computers do you think is better? I mean, what's the difference between them?

Salesman: Well, this one costs more, but it has a much better screen[16]. This part of it is made of high-quality plastic.

Woman: I only want the computer for watching movies.[17] I like to watch movies when I get home from work.

Salesman: Hmm...well, the other computer is good for the money[18]. It's much cheaper. We sell a lot of them and all our customers are satisfied with them.

Woman: Hmm...I'd like the cheaper one, please. Can I pay in cash[19]?
Salesman: Certainly.

Notes

1   Sausage Sandwiches: 夹香肠的三明治

2   There was one sausage left over.: 还剩下一根香肠。

3   care for: 喜欢

4   He wouldn't stop shaking his head: 那狗不停地摇晃着脑袋

5   properly: 稳当地

6   something that didn't agree with him: 一些不合适（不好消化）的东西

7   remembered: 想起，记起

8   You have?: 你真的吃了？这里用升调，表示惊讶。

9   Tell the doctor about the dog.: 把狗的情况告诉医生。

10 I had a very unpleasant hour with the doctor: 我在医生那儿的一个钟头折腾得很厉害

11 The medicine made me very sick.: 那个药让我很难受。

12 seemed quite well again: 似乎也康复了

13 came with the milk: 来送牛奶

14 Have you?: 是吗？

15 accident: 差错，事故

16 it has a much better screen: 这个的屏幕要好得多

17 I only want the computer for watching movies.: 我只想用电脑看电影。

18 the other computer is good for the money: 另外一台电脑价钱比较合适

19 in cash: 用现金付款

Lesson 23

Text A

The Bloody Thumb

1 **Discuss briefly the questions with your partner.**

Do you enjoy watching magic shows? Why/Why not?

2 **Listen to Text A once and answer the following questions.**

1   Where did the story take place?

_____

2   Did the author know the people there?

_____

3   Did the author enjoy his time there? Why?

_____

4   Who did the author meet at a café?

_____

3 **Listen to Text A again. Take notes and answer the questions below.**

1   Who started the conversation first?

_____

2   What did the old man say?

_____

3   How did the old man arouse the author's curiosity?

_____

4   Who was killed?

_____

5   What was the old man's best friend doing when he was attacked?

_____

6   What attacked the old man's best friend?

_____

7   How did the old man find out that his friend was killed?

_____

8   How did the old man know that it was his friend's thumb?

_____

9   What did the old man do when he finished the story?

_____

10   Why did the author pay the bill for the old man?

_____

11   What did the waiter say about the old man's story?

_____

4   **Retell the story of Text A.**

1   Form a group of three or four and retell the story together. Take turns to give sentences until the story is completed. You may choose one of the following examples as the beginning of your story.

> • John was a poor old man. Whenever he came to my café, he could always find someone to pay for his coffee.
> • I've been living in this town all my life. I always have my coffee in a café in the town, but I've never paid for it.
> • Once I was a stranger in a town. I enjoyed meeting people from all walks of life and liked listening to their stories.

2   Regroup with students from different groups in step 1. Each student retells the story from his/her previous group.

5   **Discuss the following questions in groups of three or four. After the discussion, select one member of your group to report to the class what you have talked about.**

1   Do you think the story was worth a cup of coffee? Why/Why not?
2   Do you talk to strangers when you travel by train/plane or when you eat in a restaurant? Why/Why not?
3   Have you ever been tricked by anybody? Tell your story and share the lessons you have learned from it.

Text B

The Party

1 **Listen to Text B once and answer the following questions.**

  1 Who are talking to each other?

    _____

  2 Where are they?

    _____

  3 What are they talking about?

    _____

2 **Listen to Text B again. Take notes and answer the questions below.**

  1 What is Claire Walton doing?

  2 Who is calling Claire?

  3 What is Claire going to do?

  4 Why is Mick calling?

  5 Why is Mick giving a party?

  6 When does the party start?

  7 When is Claire leaving for her holiday?

  8 Will the party go on very late?

  9 Will Claire go to the party?

 10 What sort of thing does Claire want to bring with her?

 11 Does Mick think it necessary? Why not?

 12 Why do you think Mick says goodbye to Claire in such a hurry?

    _____

13   What does Mick forget to tell Claire?

_____

3   **Describe to your partner the picture below with the following words and expressions.**

two people in the picture
talk about something pleasant
look pleased
have a happy conversation
a man
heavyset
bearded
short black hair
ordinary-looking
in a sweater
stand/sit against a bookcase
his left arm resting on the bookcase
hold the cellphone in his right hand
some cards on the wall behind him
some books on the bookcase
three jars on the bookcase
with some pens, pencils, rulers and brushes in the jars
a table lamp

a woman

good-looking

short curly hair

be well-dressed

a scarf around her neck

look happy

a fruit basket on the small table against the wall

a plant on the table

a desk with several drawers

be placed in a corner of the room

a photo frame

a vase with some roses in it

a corner of an oil painting

seem to be a nice and neat room

4 Suppose you are Claire and your partner plays the role of Mick. What do you bring to Mick when you are invited to his housewarming party?

Text C

How Did You Lose Your Way?

1 Read the following text aloud to your partner. Your partner listens to you without looking at the text.

Mrs. Brown's old grandfather lived with her and her husband. Every morning, he went for a walk in the park and came home at half past twelve for his lunch.

But one day, a police car stopped outside Mrs. Brown's house at twelve o'clock, and two policemen helped her grandfather to get out. One of them said to Mrs. Brown, "The poor old gentleman lost his way in the park and phoned us for help, so we sent a car to bring him home." Mrs. Brown was very surprised, but she thanked the policemen and they left.

"But, Grandfather," she then said, "you have been to that park nearly every day for twenty years. How did you lose your way there?"

The old man smiled, closed one eye and said, "I didn't quite lose my way. I just got tired and I didn't want to walk home!"

2 Your partner retells the story to you. Check if any information is missing in his/her retelling.

3 Tell your partner whether you would do the same as the grandfather did and what you would say to the old man and how you saw through him if you were a policeman.

Sentence-making

Pick out useful words and expressions from the following sentences and make sentences with them.

Example

I've been very busy, but I'm going away **on holiday** soon.

> ➢ Where is Peter? He is on holiday.
> ➢ I was on holiday in Spain at this time last year.
> ➢ When are you going away on holiday?

- Was there anything exciting?
- A pack of hungry dogs killed and ate my best friend.
- He was working in his olive grove on the hillside.
- The big bones were lying here and there in the grove.
- He pushed open a matchbox which he was holding in his hand.
- Please don't trouble him with it.
- Is the story worth a cup of coffee, sir?
- I'm phoning because I want to invite you to a party.
- Will the party go on very late?
- I'm looking forward to seeing you again.
- Every morning, he went for a walk in the park.
- A police car stopped outside her house.
- Two policemen helped her grandfather to get out.
- The poor old gentleman lost his way in the park.
- He phoned us for help.
- We sent a car to bring him home.

Scripts

Text A　The Bloody Thumb[1]

I met the old man at a café. I was a stranger[2] in the town.

"Did you hear the news yesterday?" he asked me.

"I didn't," I said. "Was there anything exciting?"

"Exciting, no! It was important to me and very, very sad. A pack of hungry dogs[3] killed and ate my best friend."

"Oh dear!" I cried. "I am sorry. How did it happen?"

"He was working in his olive grove[4] on the hillside[5]. The pack attacked him there. We'll never know all the facts, of course. When he didn't return, I went to his grove and…"

"You found the body?" I asked.

The old fellow[6] drank half his coffee. "The body?" he repeated. "No, no. I said they were hungry dogs, didn't I? The big bones were lying here and there in the grove.[7] But I found this." He pushed open a matchbox[8] which he was holding in his hand.

The box contained a man's thumb. It was lying on some white, bloody material. There was a cut[9]—an old cut—on the thumbnail.

"See that cut," the man said. "I recognized[10] it. This is my friend's right thumb. The dogs ate the rest of him!"

The old man began to cry then. He finished his coffee quickly and left the café. I drank mine and called the waiter.

"I'll pay the gentleman's bill[11]," I said. "Please don't trouble him with it. His poor friend…how awful! You've heard the news?"

The waiter laughed, "Yes. There's a hole at the bottom of the matchbox. He puts his own thumb through the hole. The 'blood' is red ink, I believe. Is the story worth a cup of coffee, sir?"

Text B　The Party

Claire Walton is working at home. The phone rings. It is an old friend.

Claire:　Hello.

Mick:　Hello, Claire. This is Mick.

Claire:　Mick! Nice to hear from you again.[12] How are you?

Mick:　Fine, thanks. And you?

Claire: Oh, not so bad. I've been very busy, but I'm going away on holiday[13] soon.

Mick: Good. Listen. I'm phoning because I want to invite you to a party at our new house. And...

Claire: New house? Really?

Mick: Yes. We've moved.[14] That's why we're giving the party. Can you come?

Claire: Well, that depends[15]. When is it?

Mick: This Saturday evening.

Claire: Well...I'm going away on Sunday morning. Very early. Will the party go on very late?[16]

Mick: Until two in the morning. But you don't have to stay that long. Well? What about it?

Claire: All right. I'll come. But I'd like to bring a present. Something for your new house. What would you like?

Mick: Nothing. I mean, don't bring anything. It isn't necessary.

Claire: But I'd still like...

Mick: Just bring yourself![17] I'm looking forward to seeing you again.[18] It's been a long time!

Claire: Yes, it has. I'm looking forward to seeing you, too, and your new house. Uh...when does the party start?

Mick: Come any time after eight. All right?

Claire: Yes. Oh, by the w...

Mick: Bye! See you on Saturday evening.

Claire: Wait a moment, Mick. You haven't...Mick? Are you still there?[19] You haven't given me your new address. Hello? Mick? Hello?

Notes

1   The Bloody Thumb: 血淋淋的大拇指

2   a stranger: 一个异乡人、外来客

3   A pack of hungry dogs: 一群饿狗

4   in his olive grove: 在他的橄榄树林里

5   on the hillside: 在山坡上

6   The old fellow: 这个老家伙

7   The big bones were lying here and there in the grove.: 大块的骨头四散在林子里。

8   a matchbox: 一个火柴盒

9   a cut: 一个刀印、刀痕

10   recognized: 认出来，辨认

11   I'll pay the gentleman's bill: 我来替这位先生付账

12   Nice to hear from you again.: 很高兴你打电话来。

13   going away on holiday: 外出度假

14　We've moved.: 我们搬家了。

15　that depends: 那要视情况而定

16　Will the party go on very late?: 派对要到很晚吗？

17　Just bring yourself!: 只要你来就行了！

18　I'm looking forward to seeing you again.: 期待着再次见面。

19　Are you still there?: 你还在听吗？

Lesson 24

Text A

We Are Not Deaf!

1 Discuss briefly the questions with your partner.

How do young people give parents more company when they are busy with work? What do you think family members and society should do to give more love and care to the elderly?

2 Listen to Text A once and answer the following questions.

1 How many people are there talking? Who are they?

_____

2 Where do Jane and Lise have their lunch?

_____

3 Why are the girls tired?

_____

4 When are the girls leaving?

_____

3 Listen to Text A again. Take notes and answer the questions below.

1 What is the answer from Janet when Lise says that they are leaving soon?

_____

2 Why does David want to keep the girls there longer?

_____

3 What is the reason Lise gives for leaving soon?

_____

4 Is Janet surprised to hear that? Why?

_____

5 Where are the girls staying?

_____

6   Is Lise happy about Janet's offer of going to see Malcolm?

_____

7   What's the matter with Malcolm?

_____

8   Why does David say that they are not deaf?

_____

9   Do you think David is right?

_____

4   **Retell the story of Text A.**

1   Form a group of three or four and retell the story together. Take turns to give sentences until the story is completed. You may choose one of the following examples as the beginning of your story.

> - Having finished lunch with Uncle David and Aunt Janet, I was feeling exhausted from having to shout throughout the entire meal.
> - After lunch, my two nieces, Lise and Jane, were eager to leave. I think shouting throughout the entire meal had left them exhausted.
> - Lise and Jane had just finished lunch with Uncle David and Aunt Janet. Both of them seemed tired, likely from having to shout to communicate with the elderly couple.

2   Regroup with students from different groups in step 1. Each student retells the story from his/her previous group.

5   **Discuss the following questions in groups of three or four. After the discussion, select one member of your group to report to the class what you have talked about.**

1   Use as many descriptive words as you can to describe Janet and David and their daily life.

2   Why do you think Janet and David entertained the two girls?

Text B

That Hurts a Lot.

1 **Listen to Text B once and answer the following questions.**

1　What time of the day was that?

_____

2　Where was Malc?

_____

3　What was he doing there?

_____

4　Why was Malc in the hospital?

_____

2 **Listen to Text B again. Take notes and answer the questions below.**

1　What did the doctor ask Malc to do first?

_____

2　Did the doctor want Malc to sit in a chair?

_____

3　Then what did the doctor ask Malc to do?

_____

4　Why did the doctor ask Malc to do this?

_____

5　How did Malc feel when he held up his right arm?

_____

6　Did Malc feel any pain in his legs?

_____

7　Was Malc injured seriously?

_____

8　What did the doctor want to be done?

_____

9　Could they do it right away?

_____

10　When could they do it?

_____

11　So could Malc go home immediately?

_____

3 Describe to your partner the picture below with the following words and
expressions.

in the doctor's consulting room
a bed in the room
a small table beside the bed
two small bottles on the table
a small tray and a roll of bandage on the table
a young man
tall, strong and athletic
long hair
in jeans
in his early twenties, perhaps
lie on the bed
his shirt unbuttoned
one arm in his shirt
try to raise his right arm
look painful
his legs stretching out on the bed
his left hand resting on the bed
a middle-aged doctor
be dressed in a long white overall
with long black hair
stand beside the bed

his left hand on the young man's right shoulder
his right hand holding the young man's elbow
give him a medical check-up
try to find out what is wrong with the arm

4 Have you ever gone to the Casualty Department of the hospital by yourself or with a family member? Share your experience with your partner.

Text C

At the Doctor's

1 Play the audio of the section with the marks "*" below to your partner. Your partner listens without looking at the text.

*Doctor: Good morning. How are you?
Patient: I'm very worried, Doctor.
Doctor: Oh? What are you worried about?
Patient: I'm afraid that I'm very ill.
Doctor: I'm sorry to hear that. Why do you think so?
Patient: Because I feel tired all the time, even when I wake up in the morning. I find it very difficult to do any work. I have no appetite. My wife cooks me delicious meals but I can only eat a little.
Doctor: How do you sleep?
Patient: Very badly, Doctor.
Doctor: Do you find it difficult to get to sleep, or do you wake up early?
Patient: Both, Doctor. I never get to sleep until two o'clock and I always wake up at five.
Doctor: Are you worried about anything?
Patient: Well, yes, I am. I'm worried about my work. I've just taken a new job. I earn a lot of money but it's difficult work. I'm always afraid of making a mistake.
Doctor: I see. Please take off your shirt and lie down on the couch.
Patient: Yes, Doctor.*

The doctor examines the patient.

Doctor: Well, there's nothing very much wrong with you, I'm glad to say. You're working too hard and worrying too much. Do you take much exercise?

Patient: No, Doctor. I never have enough time for exercise. I start work very early in the morning and finish late in the evening. Then I can't get to sleep. Can you give me some medicine to help me to sleep?

Doctor: I can, but I'm not going to. You don't need medicine. You need advice. Don't work so hard. Too much work is bad for you. Don't worry about your work. It's silly to worry. Take regular exercise.

Patient: But I may lose my job, Doctor! It's hard to get a job like mine.

Doctor: Then get an easier one, even if you earn less money. Which would you rather have, health or wealth?

Patient: You're right, Doctor. It's more important to be healthy than wealthy. I'll change my job. I'm grateful for your advice.

Doctor: Come and see me again in a month's time. I think you'll be a different man!

2 Your partner retells what the conversation is about. Check if any information is missing in his/her retelling.

3 Nowadays, many people live or work under pressure. Tell your partner about how you deal with pressure.

Sentence-making

Pick out useful words and expressions from the following sentences and make sentences with them.

Example

I must go back and **look after** Malcolm.

- ➢ Mum is looking after granny, who is ill.
- ➢ We must respect and look after old people.
- ➢ The children are well looked after in the nursery.

- We'll have to leave soon.
- What's the matter with him?
- Well, I'm not surprised Malcolm isn't well.
- And you don't feel any pain anywhere else? In your legs, for example.
- It's probably nothing serious.
- But I think we'd better have that shoulder X-rayed.
- So it'd be better if you stayed in hospital for the night.
- What are you worried about?
- I'm always afraid of making a mistake.
- It's more important to be healthy than wealthy.
- I'm grateful for your advice.

Scripts

Text A   We Are Not Deaf!

Jane and Lise have had lunch with Uncle David and Aunt Janet. The two old people are deaf, and the girls are tired because they have to shout[1]. They both want to leave.

Lise: We'll have to leave soon, Aunt Janet.

Aunt Janet:　Yes, of course you can have some tea, dear. I'll go and make some.[2]

Jane:　Oh no, Lise. Stop her! You'd better say it louder.[3]

Lise:　WE'LL HAVE TO LEAVE, AUNT JANET.

Uncle David: You can't leave yet. I want to hear some more about Canada.[4]

Lise:　But I must go back and look after Malcolm. Oh dear[5], they can't hear. I MUST GO BACK AND LOOK AFTER MALCOLM.

Aunt Janet:　Why? What's the matter with him?[6]

Lise:　I TOLD YOU, AUNT JANET. HE ISN'T WELL.

Aunt Janet:　But I thought you said he was in the hotel[7]. Where are you staying?

Lise:　We're camping...WE'RE CAMPING.

Aunt Janet:　In this weather? Well, I'm not surprised Malcolm isn't well.[8] Perhaps I ought to come out and see him.

Lise:　NO, THAT'S NOT A GOOD IDEA, AUNTIE. HE'S ILL.

Uncle David: What's the matter with him?

Lise:　He's got a cold.

Jane:　He's got a temperature.

Lise:　Oh, what's the use? HE'S GOT A COLD.

Uncle David: All right, all right, we can hear. We're not deaf!

Text B　That Hurts a Lot.

Malc went to the Casualty Department[9] of the hospital. There he was examined by a doctor.

Doctor: Right. Just take off your jacket and shirt. And lie down[10] on that bed over there. That's right. Now, just hold up your right arm[11], will you? Does this hurt?[12]

Malc:　No.

Doctor: And this?

Malc:　Yes, a bit[13]. Ouch![14]

Doctor: And do you feel anything when I do this?

Malc:　Yes, that hurts quite a lot[15].

Doctor: And you don't feel any pain anywhere else? In your legs, for example.

Malc:　No, nothing.

Doctor: Well, it's probably nothing serious. But I think we'd better have that shoulder X-rayed[16]. We can't do that until morning, though. So it'd be better if you stayed in hospital for the night.

Notes

1   have to shout: 不得不大声喊

2   make some (tea): 泡点（茶）

3   You'd better say it louder.: 你最好大点声说。

4   I want to hear some more about Canada.: 我想多了解点加拿大的情况。

5   Oh dear: 天哪

6   Why? What's the matter with him?: 啊唷！他怎么啦？此处 why 表示惊奇。

7   he was in the hotel: 他住在旅馆里

8   I'm not surprised Malcolm isn't well.: 马尔科姆身体不适，我一点也不奇怪。

9   the Casualty Department: 急救科

10   lie down: 躺下

11   hold up your right arm: 举起你的右臂

12   Does this hurt?: 这样疼吗？

13   a bit: 有一点（疼）

14   Ouch!: 哎哟! 疼痛时的叫喊。

15   that hurts quite a lot: 这样很疼

16   have that shoulder X-rayed: 给那只肩膀拍 X 光照片

Lesson 25

Text A

A Pocketful of Pigs

1 **Discuss briefly the questions with your partner.**

What do you think of the change in payment methods? What do you think of the online payment?

2 **Listen to Text A once and answer the following questions.**

1　What is the text about?

_____

2　What do you learn from it?

_____

_____

3 **Listen to Text A again. Take notes and answer the questions below.**

1　Did money exist from the very beginning of human civilization?

_____

2　How did people "buy" things when there was no money?

_____

3　Give some examples of the trade at that time in the text.

_____

4　What problems did the trade at that time have?

_____

5　How did people solve these problems?

_____

6　Why does the text say "a pocketful of money was better than a pocketful of pigs"?

_____

7　What are the advantages of using money?

_____

4 Retell the story of Text A.

1   Form a group of three or four and retell the story together. Take turns to give sentences until the story is completed. You may choose one of the following examples as the beginning of your story.

> • Once upon a time, there was no money. Everything was used as a substitute for money.
> • A long time ago, if people wanted to get something, they had to give something. This is the way people bought things.

2   Regroup with students from different groups in step 1. Each student retells the story from his/her previous group.

5 Discuss the following questions in groups of three or four. After the discussion, select one member of your group to report to the class what you have talked about.

1   What would our present-day life be like if we didn't have money?
2   Name the online payment methods you know. How do you think people will trade in a future of rapid technological advance?

Text B

Let's Play Chess.

1 Listen to Text B once and answer the following questions.

1   Who are involved in this dialogue?

_____

2   What is the possible relationship between them?

_____

3   Where are they?

_____

4   What are they doing?

_____

2 **Listen to Text B again. Take notes and answer the questions below.**

1   Who suggests that they play chess?

_____

2   Does Mr. Dawson often play chess?

_____

3   Has Mr. Wilson learned to play chess for a long time?

_____

4   How do they get a board to play?

_____

5   Is Mr. Dawson a good player?

_____

6   Did Mr. Dawson win any prize before? What prize was it?

_____

7   Did Mr. Wilson win any prize? What prize was it?

_____

8   When did Mr. Wilson win his prize?

_____

9   Who is a better player, Mr. Dawson or Mr. Wilson?

_____

3 **Describe to your partner the picture below with the following words and expressions.**

a common room

a bookshelf standing against one side of the room

some books on the shelf

a chessboard near the door

some chessmen on the board

sit on a chair at one side of the board

sit on the opposite side of the board

face the door

his turn to move

be dressed in a white shirt

wear a tie

rest one's elbow on the board

think very hard about his next move

4 **Suppose you are Mr. Dawson and your partner plays the role of Mr. Wilson. What do you say when you are invited to play chess with him? And tell him how you feel when he turns out to be a very good player.**

Text C

Can I Get My Money Back?

1 **Play the audio of the following text to your partner. Your partner listens without looking at the text.**

Man: I'm not satisfied with it.

Saleswoman: Why not? What's wrong with it?

Man: Sometimes it goes fast. And sometimes it goes slow. And the alarm doesn't work, either.

Saleswoman: Would you like another one?

Man: No. Can I have my money back?

Saleswoman: Hmm...have you got a receipt?

Man: A receipt?

Saleswoman: Yes. I must see your receipt. You can't have your money back

	without a receipt.
Man:	Oh, I'm not certain, but I think I've lost it.

2 **Your partner retells what the conversation is about. Check if any information is missing in his/her retelling.**

3 **Tell your partner what you will do if you find what you buy unsatisfactory or of poor quality and why you do that.**

Sentence-making

Pick out useful words and expressions from the following sentences and make sentences with them.

Example

This is the way it used to be.

> This is the way I cook vegetables.
> This is the way he speaks.
> Is this the way you treat your friends?

* I will give you my cow for your pig.
* But they had to work out a good trade, one that came out even.
* It was too hard to carry around all the things for trading.
* People had to take too much time to get things they needed.
* Money could "stand for" apples, or bowls, or pigs.
* People could buy things with the money they got from work.
* Mr. Wilson and Mr. Dawson are watching some men playing chess.
* Those two men have already finished playing.
* My prize was for the best player in the country.
* Now let's start playing chess seriously.
* I'm not satisfied with it.
* Can I have my money back?
* You can't have your money back without a receipt.

Scripts

Text A   A Pocketful of[1] Pigs

Once there was no money.

If people wanted to get something, they had to give something. This is the way it used to be.[2]

"I will give you my cow for your pig[3]," a man would say.

"I'll give you my bowl if you give me a shirt," another would say. "Here are seven oranges for one fish."

"Will you give me a chicken for a bag of corn[4]?"

People had to trade[5] things every day. They had to give a thing to get a thing because there wasn't any money.

But they had to work out a good trade, one that came out even[6].

What could you get for two chickens? Were three bags of apples a good trade for two bags of grapes? Or one bag of apples for a little butter? What was an even trade?[7] It was hard to know.

And it was too hard to carry around[8] all the things for trading. People had to take too much time to get things they needed. So they thought of a new way to trade.

They thought of money.

Money could "stand for[9]" apples, or bowls, or pigs.

And a pocketful of money was better than a pocketful of pigs.

With money, it was not so hard to trade. Everyone could use money. The man who needed a pig could buy it with money. The man who sold the pig could keep the money until he needed something. People could work for money, and people could buy things with the money they got from work.

Text B   Let's Play Chess[10].

Mr. Wilson and Mr. Dawson are watching some men playing chess.

Mr. Wilson: Dawson, let's play chess.

Mr. Dawson: I haven't played chess for a long time.

Mr. Wilson: That's all right. I'm a beginner[11]. I've just learned how to play.

Mr. Dawson: Look, there's a chessboard[12]. Those two men have already finished playing.

After they have played for a few minutes.

Mr. Wilson:　You're a very good player.

Mr. Dawson:　Not really, but once I won a prize[13].

Mr. Wilson:　So did I. I won a prize last week but it was a prize for beginners.

Mr. Dawson:　My prize was for the best player in the country. Now let's start playing chess seriously.[14]

Notes

1　A Pocketful of: 满满一口袋

2　This is the way it used to be.: 从前就是这样的。

3　I will give you my cow for your pig: 我用我的母牛换你的猪

4　a bag of corn: 一袋玉米

5　trade: 交易

6　came out even: 结果是公平的

7　What was an even trade?: 什么是公平交易呢？

8　carry around: 随身带着

9　stand for: 代表，代替

10　Play Chess: 下国际象棋

11　a beginner: 一个初学者

12　a chessboard: 一个棋盘

13　but once I won a prize: 但我曾经得过奖

14　Now let's start playing chess seriously.: 现在让我们开始认真下棋吧。

Lesson 26

Text A

The Stage Fright

1 **Discuss briefly the questions with your partner.**

Have you ever tried to play any musical instrument? Why/Why not?

2 **Listen to Text A once and answer the following questions.**

1 What is the story about?

_____

2 What musical instrument did Tom play?

_____

3 What happened at the recital? Was it Tom's first recital?

_____

3 **Listen to Text A again. Take notes and answer the questions below.**

1 Did Tom practice very hard before the recital?

_____

2 Why did Tom practice so hard?

_____

3 Why did Tom's teacher say that he was gifted?

_____

4 Why was Tom very anxious before he went onto the stage?

_____

5 How did Tom feel when he stood up to go to the piano?

_____

6 Did Tom's family encourage him? How?

_____

7 What did Tom do to calm himself down after he had sat down at the piano?

_____

8　What happened after Tom had played the first five bars of his music?

_____

9　Why did Tom start over again?

_____

10　Did Tom finish the piece of music?

_____

11　How did Tom leave the stage?

_____

12　How did Tom feel at that moment? Why?

_____

13　Would he continue his musical career after the recital?

_____

4 **Retell the story of Text A.**

1　Form a group of three or four and retell the story together. Take turns to give sentences until the story is completed. You may choose one of the following examples as the beginning of your story.

> - Tom was a student in a music school. He was the best student in the whole class.
> - Tom had been working for the piano recital for weeks on end. He didn't want to disappoint his teacher and his family.
> - Since it was the first time that Tom played at a recital, his grandparents, aunt, and uncle all came to hear him play. They sat in the audience, waiting for his turn to play.

2　Regroup with students from different groups in step 1. Each student retells the story from his/her previous group.

5 **Discuss the following questions in groups of three or four. After the discussion, select one member of your group to report to the class what you have talked about.**

1　Use as many descriptive words as you can to describe Tom and the piano recital.

2　Would you continue your musical career after the recital if you were Tom? Why?

Text B

I Shall Never Fly Again.

1 **Listen to Text B once and answer the following questions.**

1   How many people are engaged in this dialogue? Who are they?

2   What are they talking about?

2 **Listen to Text B again. Take notes and answer the questions below.**

1   Where is Charles going for his holidays?

2   How long is Charles going to stay there?

3   Who is Charles going to visit?

4   Does Tom also want to go to Australia?

5   How is Charles going to Australia?

6   Why isn't Charles going to Australia by sea?

7   How did Tom go to Singapore?

8   How did Tom like the flight?

9   What happened during the flight?

10   What did the crew do?

11   What did the pilot ask the people at the airport to tell him?

12   Did the plane land safely?

3 Describe to your partner the picture below with the following words and expressions.

at the airport

a passenger plane

three men walking to the ramp

walk with big strides

board the plane

be dressed in an overcoat

hold a briefcase in his left hand

a big suitcase

wear a hat

in a hurry

two teenagers

a light-colored pullover

dark-colored trousers

look at the passengers

with his hands in his pockets

point to the passengers

talk about traveling

4 Suppose you are Charles and your partner plays the role of Tom. Talk about one of your most interesting/unforgettable holidays.

Text C

Never Give Up!

1 **Read the section with the marks "*" below aloud to your partner. Your partner listens to you without looking at the text.**

*It was a dark day when we got our report cards. The sky was full of gray clouds and it was sprinkling rain. I was over to Clyde's house, and Gloria and Kitty were there. Sam probably would have been there, too. Only he had got a two-week job in the afternoons helping out at Freddie's. Actually he only did it so that his mother would let him be on the track team again. Sam and his mother had this little system going.

Clyde's report card was on the kitchen table and we all sat around it like it was some kind of a big important document. I had got a pretty good report card and had wanted to show it off, but I knew it wasn't the time.

Clyde pushed the card toward me and I read it. He had all satisfactory remarks on the side labeled Personal Traits and Behavior. He had also received a B in music and art appreciation. But everything else was either a C or a D except mathematics. His mathematics mark was a big red F that had been circled. I don't know why they had to circle the F when it was the only red mark on the card. In the Teacher's Comments section, someone had written that Clyde had "little ability to handle an academic program."*

"A little ability is better than none," I said. No one said anything, so I figured it probably wasn't the right time to try to cheer Clyde up. I knew all about his switching from a commercial program to an academic program, but I really hadn't thought he'd have any trouble. "I saw the grade advisor today. He said I should switch back to the commercial program." Clyde looked like he'd start crying any minute. His eyes were red and his voice was shaky. "He said that I had to take mathematics over and if I failed again or failed another required subject, I couldn't graduate. The way it is now I'm going to have to finish up in the summer because I switched over."

"I think you can pass it if you really want to," Clyde's sister, Kitty, said. Just then Clyde's mother came in and she gave a quick look at Kitty.

"Hi, young ladies and young gentlemen." Mrs. Jones was a kind of heavy woman but she was pretty. You could tell she was Kitty's mother if you looked close. She put her package down and started taking things out.

"I heard you people talking when I first came in. By the way you hushed up, I guess you don't want me to hear what you were talking about. I'll be out of your way in a minute as soon as I put the frozen foods in the refrigerator."

"I got my report card today," Clyde said. His mother stopped taking the foods out and turned toward us. Clyde pushed the report card about two inches toward her. She really didn't even have to look at the card to know that it was bad. She could have told that just by looking at Clyde. But she picked it up and looked at it for a long time. First she looked at one side and then the other and then back at the first side again.

"What did they say around the school?" she asked, still looking at the card.

"They said I should drop the academic course and go back to the other one." I could hardly hear Clyde, because he spoke so low.

"Well, what are you going to do, young man?" She looked up at Clyde and Clyde looked up at her, and there were tears in his eyes and I almost started crying. I can't stand to see my friends cry. "What are you going to do, Mr. Jones?"

"I'm…I'm going to keep the academic course," Clyde said. "Do you think it's going to be any easier this time?" Mrs. Jones asked.

"No."

"Things ain't always easy." For a minute, there was a faraway look in her eyes, but then her face turned into a big smile. "You're just like your father, boy. That man never would give up on anything he really wanted. Did l ever tell you he was trying to learn to play the trombone?"

"No." Clyde still had tears in his eyes, but he was smiling, too. Suddenly everybody was happy. It was like seeing a rainbow when it was still raining.

2 Your partner retells what he/she has heard. Check if any information is missing in his/her retelling.

3 Tell your partner what your parents will do if they learn that your school performance is not as good as expected.

Sentence-making

Pick out useful words and expressions from the following sentences and make sentences with them.

Example

It **takes** more time **to** go by sea.

> The work took us a week to finish.
> It took them at least one month to repair the machine.
> It will take several years to build this magnificent building.

- Tom was sick with disappointment.
- The piano recital had turned out well, all except for his solo.
- He had given up sports until after the recital.
- He wanted to make his parents proud of him.
- He spent all his time with the piano.
- His grandparents, aunt, and uncle all came to hear him play.
- He was anxious to show them that he was the best in the whole class.
- He looked into the audience and saw his family smiling back at him.
- His mouth went dry.
- He sat down at the piano.
- Where are you going for your holidays, Charles?
- I once went to Singapore by air.
- One of the engines caught fire.
- I was over to Clyde's house.
- A little ability is better than none.
- His mother stopped taking the foods out.
- I can't stand to see my friends cry.
- That man never would give up on anything he really wanted.

Scripts

Text A   The Stage Fright[1]

Tom was sick with disappointment[2]. The piano recital had turned out well[3], all except for his solo[4]. He couldn't understand how it could have happened. He had practiced for weeks that seemed like months.[5] He had given up sports until after the recital because he wanted to make his parents proud of him. He spent all his time with the piano.

His teacher had said he was gifted[6]. It was true that he accepted music as another language, another way to talk to people.[7] His grandparents, aunt, and uncle all came to hear him play, and he was anxious to show them that he was the best in the whole class.

But, when he stood up to go to the piano, his knees felt weak[8]. He looked into the audience and saw his family smiling back at him. His mouth went dry.[9] His fingers began to tremble. The trembling became uncontrollable shaking as though he had caught a bad cold.

He sat down at the piano[10]. He took a deep breath[11]. He played the first five bars[12] of his music, then realized with horror that he had forgotten the rest. He started over, thinking that would help.[13] It didn't. He stood up as if in slow motion[14] and walked off the stage. He was a failure. The demon stage fright had left a brilliant musical career in ruins[15].

Text B   I Shall Never Fly Again.

Tom Jackson and Charles Brown are talking about their summer holidays.

Tom: Where are you going for your holidays, Charles?

Charles: To Australia. I'm going to visit my uncle in Brisbane[16] for three weeks.

Tom: Good gracious![17] You certainly are lucky. How are you going there?

Charles: By air[18], of course. It takes more time to go by sea[19].

Tom: I once[20] went to Singapore by air. It was very exciting, but never again[21].

Charles: Why? Did you feel frightened?

Tom: For a short time. One of the engines caught fire[22].

Charles: What did the crew do?

Tom: They put it out[23] and the pilot flew the airplane back to the airport. Then he asked the people at the airport where the emergency runway[24] was.

Charles: Did you land safely?

Tom: Yes, we did. But I shall never fly again.

Notes

1 The Stage Fright: 舞台恐惧症，怯场

2 was sick with disappointment: 由于失望而懊丧

3 turned out well: 结果很好

4 except for his solo: 除了他的独奏之外

5 He had practiced for weeks that seemed like months.: 他练习了几个星期，但是感觉有几个月那么长。

6 gifted: 有天赋的，才华横溢的

7 It was true that he accepted music as another language, another way to talk to people.: 确实，他把音乐看成是另一种语言，另一种与人交流的方式。

8 his knees felt weak: 他的膝盖发软

9 His mouth went dry.: 他的嘴发干。

10 sat down at the piano: 在钢琴前坐下

11 took a deep breath: 深深地吸了一口气

12 the first five bars: 前五个小节

13 He started over, thinking that would help.: 他重新开始弹，以为这样能帮他（记起乐谱）。

14 in slow motion: 慢动作

15 had left a brilliant musical career in ruins: 使他辉煌的音乐生涯毁于一旦

16 Brisbane: 布里斯班，澳大利亚昆士兰州首府

17 Good gracious!: 天哪!

18 By air: 乘飞机

19 by sea: 乘海轮

20 once: 曾经

21 but never again: 但再也不（乘飞机）了

22 caught fire: 着火了

23 put it out: 把火扑灭

24 the emergency runway: 应急跑道

Lesson 27

Text A

They Threatened Me with a Knife.

1 **Discuss briefly the questions with your partner.**

Have you ever seen a robbery or any other crimes? Describe what you have seen to your partner.

2 **Listen to Text A once and answer the following questions.**

1　What is the story about?

2　How many people are involved in the story? Who are they?

3 **Listen to Text A again. Take notes and answer the questions below.**

1　When did the burglary happen?

2　Do you think the man was too careless?

3　Why did the man open the door without thinking?

4　Who were at the door?

5　What did they do?

6　Why didn't the man have a good look at them?

7　What did the two burglars take?

8   Why did they leave in a hurry?

_____

9   Who released the man?

_____

10   Did the police inspector make a promise? What did he say?

_____

4 **Retell the story of Text A.**

1   Form a group of three or four and retell the story together. Take turns to give sentences until the story is completed. You may choose one of the following examples as the beginning of your story.

> • Two hours ago, I was sitting in the living room and watching television. Suddenly someone knocked on the door.
> • Tonight, I was on the night duty, and received a call about a burglary, then I headed to the scene.
> • Two hours ago, Mr. Lee experienced a harrowing incident. Someone knocked on the door and he opened it without thinking.

2   Regroup with students from different groups in step 1. Each student retells the story from his/her previous group.

5 **Discuss the following questions in groups of three or four. After the discussion, select one member of your group to report to the class what you have talked about.**

1   What would you do if someone broke into your house when you were alone at home?
2   If you see someone committing a crime, how do you stop it while keeping yourself safe?

Text B

Three Wishes

1 **Listen to Text B once and answer the following questions.**

1   What is the story about?

_____

2 How many people are there in the story?

_____

3 What do you learn from the story?

_____

2 Listen to Text B again. Take notes and answer the questions below.

1 Where did the woodman and his wife live?

_____

2 What did the woodman do every day?

_____

3 What happened one day when the woodman was about to chop down a big tree?

_____

4 Who was talking to the woodman?

_____

5 What did the fairy promise to do?

_____

6 How was the woodman when he got home that evening?

_____

7 When did his wife say supper would be ready?

_____

8 What did the woodman say loudly to himself?

_____

9 What happened then?

_____

10 Was the woodman's wife surprised?

_____

11 Why did the woodman's wife become angry?

_____

12 What did the woodman's wife say then?

_____

13 Where was the black sausage then?

_____

14 What did the couple do in the end?

_____

15 What did the couple actually get from the three wishes granted by the fairy?

_____

3 Describe to your partner the picture below with the following words and expressions.

at the dinner table
at dinner time
set the table
a tablecloth
be ready for dinner
a middle-aged lady
stand by the table
wear a bonnet
in a long dress
wear a pair of glasses
with freckles on one's cheeks
be amazed at sth.
stare at the nose
be greatly surprised
a man opposite the lady
with a thick beard
have a terribly long nose
a long and protruding nose
look like a black sausage
a small man with a big belly
wear a belt/waistband
sit on a chair
talk with sb.

remove sth.
have difficulty in
get rid of

4 Suppose you are the woodman and your partner plays the role of the woodman's wife. Talk about what happened in the wood and what wishes you would want to have.

Text C

My Uncle

1 Read the section with the marks "*" below aloud to your partner. Your partner listens to you without looking at the text.

*Now I know why birds sit on telephone lines. They listen.

I am either nine or ten years old. At the orphanage they call me Miguel.

When I want to feel important, I say, "Call me Don Miguel."

I used to act important all the time because I felt I wasn't.

Back then, no one liked me very much because I didn't like other people.

But last year, I began to learn two important things: I was learning to see, not just look. And I was learning to listen, not just hear.

I used to lie in the dark and make up relatives that I didn't have. My favorite relative was a nice old man who spoke Spanish, like me.

One day, a man came to see me. He said he was my uncle.

"I don't have an uncle," I said.

"Now you do," he said.

He was an old man who liked children. He had a boy once who went to South Korea. His daughter moved to the city. He said the city can be a difficult place to live in. He taught me how to see and listen. I don't know if he is my uncle or not; neither did he, but he came to see me often. I guess if you act like an uncle all the time, you are one.*

I was not a good student before my uncle came along. He took me for a walk in the fields. At one point, he spread his arms and said, "It is all here."

"What?" I said.

"Everything you need to know," he replied.

At first, it appeared to be nothing more than just a few trees. I thought I was nowhere. Then he had me close my eyes. First, I heard the breeze in the grass, then in the trees. I also heard a faraway train and a barking dog. For a while, I heard nothing. I was almost scared. He asked me to listen harder.

I heard my heart beat.

Because I used to be so sad, I had almost forgotten that I had a heart.

Once I asked him who he was.

"An experimenter," he said.

"What kind of experimenter?" I said.

He grinned and said, "Nobody knows. Like you, there is no one in the world like me. So who is to say what I will be."

One day, in the field he showed me the way the breeze made the trees move. The rustling of the leaves made a sound that frightened a nearby bird. It flew away.

We watched the bird drop an acorn.

"The bird," he said, "can make a seed move. From that seed the oak can grow fifty feet tall. It will be a friend to those who want one."

I always knew that trees were there, but I never knew they were real like me.

One Sunday, I was angry. When my uncle came, I said: "I don't have anything. I wish I had something."

"You have everything worth having," he said. "And I will give you even more. I will give some secrets of the universe. Do you believe me?"

"Yes," I said, wanting to believe him.

He gave me three small seeds.

"Put each seed into a small box filled with dirt. Then care for them. Talk to them if you wish. They will grow with you."

Now they are in larger boxes. One of the plants has grown up to my knee. I sometimes wonder what else it is up to.

Another time, we were walking in the field when we saw two birds on a telephone line. They seemed so peaceful. Then suddenly they flew away. My uncle just laughed.

"See," he said. "Someone said something they didn't like. Be careful what you tell the birds."

One night, I passed by the office of the orphanage. A man I don't like very much was on the phone. He was angry and loud.

When he left, I went into the office and picked up the phone. I heard the funniest sound.

"Listen," I said. "Listen, birds. Come back. Never mind what he says. We like you."

One day, my uncle did not come. I waited and waited but he did not come. The man I don't like at the orphanage said my uncle was sick.

"May I go and see him?" I asked.

"No," he said. "He may be contagious."

"May I call him?"

"No," he said. "I'll call him for you."

"Don't do that," I said.

"Why not?"

"You'll make the birds fly away."

I sneaked into the office one night and called uncle.

"Are you all right?" I asked.

"Yes, but I must go away."

"Why?"

"To make room for something else."

"Will you come back?"

"I will help you remember me, if you want me to."

"I do...I do..."

When I went to bed at night, I would try to imagine that he was there. He was harder and harder to see. One night, he was not there at all. There was only a green field.

I went back to our field. It was raining. The sky was dark. I looked for uncle everywhere. I called his name.

I was angry for a while. I said some things out loud that I shouldn't have said. Two birds flew out of the tree. I made them get wet.

On the way back, I saw something that was only an inch or two tall. It was where that bird dropped the acorn. I didn't tell anybody, but I knew.

Someday uncle will be fifty feet tall.

2 Your partner retells what he/she has heard. Check if any information is missing in his/her retelling.

3 Tell your partner a story about the person who once gave you very valuable advice on your life and future development.

Sentence-making

Pick out useful words and expressions from the following sentences and make sentences with them.

Example

Once upon a time, there lived a woodman and his wife.

> ➤ Once upon a time, there lived a man called Rip van Winkle.
> ➤ Once upon a time, there was a small tribe in the deep forest.

- One of them threatened me with a knife.
- They don't seem to have done much damage to the flat.
- They lived in a cottage on the edge of a forest.
- He was about to strike the tree with the ax.
- I will grant you and your wife three wishes.
- He was feeling very hungry and could not wait for his supper.
- I wish I had a big black sausage to eat right now.
- The only thing to do was to wish it on the table again, which the woodman did.
- I used to lie in the dark and make up relatives that I didn't have.
- The city can be a difficult place to live in.
- He had me close my eyes.
- He showed me the way the breeze made the trees move.
- You have everything worth having.
- I sometimes wonder what else it is up to.
- I went into the office and picked up the phone.
- You'll make the birds fly away.
- To make room for something else.

Scripts

Text A They Threatened Me with a Knife.

Police Inspector: Good evening, sir. I understand that you have been robbed.

Mr. Lee: I certainly have.

Police Inspector: When did this happen?

Mr. Lee: About two hours ago.

Police Inspector: Why didn't you report it before?

Mr. Lee: I couldn't. I was bound and gagged.[1]

Police Inspector: Please tell me exactly what happened.

Mr. Lee: I was sitting in this room and watching television when someone knocked on the door. Without thinking, I opened it.

Police Inspector: That wasn't very wise, sir.

Mr. Lee: I know. I was expecting my wife, you see, and thought it was her.

Police Inspector: You should never open a door without looking to see who it is.

Mr. Lee: Yes, I know. I regret it very much.

Police Inspector: What happened?

Mr. Lee: Two men pushed into the flat. One of them threatened me with a knife[2] while the other bound and gagged me.

Police Inspector: Did you get a good look at them?

Mr. Lee: I'm afraid not. They were both wearing stockings over their faces.[3]

Police Inspector: What did they take?

Mr. Lee: My wallet, with $200 in it, my wristwatch, some of my wife's jewellery from our bedroom, and a silver photo frame.

Police Inspector: They don't seem to have done much damage to the flat.

Mr. Lee: No. They had just begun to search when the dogs next door began to bark. They ran off, and left me bound and gagged. It was some time before my wife returned and released me. I phoned the police at once.

Police Inspector: My men began searching the area as soon as we received your call. We'll certainly do our best to recover your property.

Text B Three Wishes

Once upon a time[4], there lived a woodman and his wife. They were very poor, and they lived in a cottage on the edge of a forest[5]. Every day, the woodman would set out early in the morning to chop down trees. As the woodman was traveling through the forest one day, he saw a fine old oak tree. "That will make plenty of planks[6]," he thought, as he felt the blade of his ax[7] to make sure it was sharp. He was about to strike the tree with the ax, when he heard someone crying out: "Please don't hurt this tree."

The woodman looked around and saw a tiny fairy[8]. "If you do not hurt this tree," she said, "I will grant you and your wife three wishes.[9]"

"I won't hurt the tree," said the woodman kindly. Then the fairy vanished!

That evening, the woodman walked slowly home. He was feeling very hungry and could not wait for his supper.[10]

"Is my supper ready?" the woodman asked his wife.

"Not for at least two hours[11]," replied his wife. So the woodman sat on a chair by the fire.

"I wish I had a big black sausage to eat right now," he said out loud. And suddenly, a delicious sausage appeared on the table before him! "Why has that black sausage suddenly appeared?" the woodman's wife asked.

So the woodman told his wife the story about the fairy. But his wife was very angry. "You have wasted the first of our wishes," she said crossly[12]. "I wish that sausage were on your nose![13]"

And with that, the sausage jumped up and stuck fast on the woodman's nose[14]. His wife could not pull it off and nor could he, so the only thing to do was to wish it on the table again, which the woodman did[15].

What a waste of three wishes! The only thing the woodman had was a good supper of black sausage.

Notes

1   I was bound and gagged.: 我被绑起来，嘴也堵上了。

2   One of them threatened me with a knife: 其中一人拿着刀恐吓我

3   They were both wearing stockings over their faces.: 他们俩脸上都套了长丝袜。

4   Once upon a time: 从前，用于讲故事的开头，尤其是童话

5   they lived in a cottage on the edge of a forest: 他们住在森林边上的一座小房子里

6   That will make plenty of planks: 那可以锯好多木板

7   as he felt the blade of his ax: 他一边试着斧头的刃

8   a tiny fairy: 一个小仙女

9   I will grant you and your wife three wishes.: 我将满足你和你妻子的三个愿望。

10   He was feeling very hungry and could not wait for his supper.: 他感觉很饿，都来不及等到晚饭了。

11   Not for at least two hours: 至少两小时后（晚饭）才能好

12   crossly: 怒气冲冲地，生气地

13   I wish that sausage were on your nose!: 我希望那香肠长在你鼻子上！

14   the sausage jumped up and stuck fast on the woodman's nose: 香肠跳起来，牢牢地粘在了樵夫的鼻子上

15   the only thing to do was to wish it on the table again, which the woodman did: 唯一能做的就是愿这香肠回到桌子上去，樵夫也的确这样做了

Lesson 28

Text A

Do You Know Who I Am?

1 **Discuss briefly the questions with your partner.**

Are you good at socializing? Why/Why not? What will you do if you are at a banquet sitting next to someone you do not know?

2 **Listen to Text A once and answer the following questions.**

1 What is the story about?

_____

2 What kind of man is Mr. Smith?

_____

3 What do you think of the secretary's wife?

_____

3 **Listen to Text A again. Take notes and answer the questions below.**

1 Why is Mr. Smith well known?

_____

2 Why does Mr. Smith like to attend various social functions?

_____

3 Does Mr. Smith accept every invitation?

_____

4 Did Mr. Smith know the hostess who invited him to the fashionable banquet?

_____

5 How did Mr. Smith feel when he received the invitation?

_____

6 How many people were invited to the banquet?

_____

7 Did Mr. Smith know those he spoke to?

_____

8 Who did the woman ask Mr. Smith about?

_____

9 Who was the gray-haired man at the end of the table?

_____

10 What was the woman's response to Mr. Smith's comments on the secretary?

_____

11 Who did the woman say she was?

_____

12 Why do you think the woman told Mr. Smith who she was?

_____

13 Why did Mr. Smith ask if the woman knew who he was?

_____

14 Why do you think Mr. Smith left the table in a hurry?

_____

4 Retell the story of Text A.

1 Form a group of three or four and retell the story together. Take turns to give sentences until the story is completed. You may choose one of the following examples as the beginning of your story.

> • Mr. Smith is very interested in social occasions. He accepted every invitation unless he was ill.
> • My husband is the Secretary of the Interior. One day at a banquet, I sat beside a man I had never met before.
> • At a banquet, I happened to overhear a conversation between a dignified woman and a funny little man.

2 Regroup with students from different groups in step 1. Each student retells the story from his/her previous group.

5 Discuss the following questions in groups of three or four. After the discussion, select one member of your group to report to the class what you have talked about.

1 How do you like the secretary's wife?
2 Have you ever made any blunders on social occasions? Share one of your experiences.
3 What do you think of party animals?
4 Do you think attending various social functions helps expand one's circle of friends? Why?

Text B

Hands Up!

1 **Listen to Text B once and answer the following questions.**

1   What was the conversation about?

2   What did the man and the woman want to do in the shop?

3   Do you think the salesman was too incautious?

2 **Listen to Text B again. Take notes and answer the questions below.**

1   Who did the woman say she wanted to buy a watch for?

2   What did the man say the watch should be?

3   What watch did the salesman show them?

4   Was this watch satisfactory to them?

5   Why was the salesman reluctant to show them the best watch in the shop?

6   Where was the best watch kept?

7   Did the salesman ask the two customers to go together with him?

8   What do you think the two customers really were?

9   Why did the manager say he couldn't open the safe?

10   Do you think the manager was being humorous?

3 **Describe to your partner the picture below with the following words and expressions.**

two burglars
burglarize
break into
in a manager's office
a big safe in the corner
a landscape painting on the wall
face the door
look scared/frightened/shocked
wear a suit and tie
stand with hands up
stand shivering/trembling
stand with one's back to the door
cut off one's way to escape
stand in the doorway
a woman with permed hair
be decently dressed
disguise oneself as
pretend to do sth.
disguise one's voice
point one's pistol at sb.
order sb. to do sth.
shout at sb.
threaten sb. with death

threaten to do sth.

keep quiet

run the risk of being caught

set off the burglar alarm

protect sb. from sth.

4 Suppose you are the shop manager and your partner plays the role of a newly employed salesperson. Talk about what to do in the face of a burglary and what precautions should be taken.

Text C

Henry's Life

1 Read the section with the marks "*" below aloud to your partner. Your partner listens to you without looking at the text.

*Henry D. Penrose was a dog with a pedigree. He lived in a fine stone house with white marble steps and red velvet drapes on every window.

His owner, Professor Randolph Penrose, was quite rich.

Each morning, Henry was driven to Obedience School in a long black limousine.

Each afternoon, he was fed two grilled lamb chops for lunch.

Each evening, he fell asleep in his fur-lined basket in front of the fireplace.

On Saturdays, he was groomed at Miss Fifi's Shop. And on Sundays, he accompanied the professor to the park, where a classical orchestra played soothing music and the grass was cool and fragrant.

Professor Penrose would stroke Henry's shiny coat and say, "You have the life, Henry, my boy!"

And Henry certainly had to agree.

Then one day, it all changed. Just like that.*

Professor Penrose received a phone call offering him a chance to dig for dinosaur bones in Idaho for one entire year.

There was only one problem. The call stated quite firmly: NO PETS ALLOWED!

The cook, Mrs. Washburn, agreed to take Henry to her home until the professor returned.

Professor Penrose hated to send Henry to live on the other side of the city. There were no marble steps or red velvet drapes on Mrs. Washburn's property.

But Henry was buttoned into his red plaid coat and driven to the Washburn's residence.

Henry stepped out of the limousine. He was so shocked that his ears stuck out like two car doors.

Such an untidy home he had never seen. It was all he could do to maintain a sense of dignity.

He was picking his way through the toys on the muddy front steps when a tumble of children spilled onto the porch, scooped him up, and before you could say "one—two", Henry was deposited in a sea of soap bubbles in the Washburn's bathtub.

Each time he tried to jump out, little hands pushed him back in.

"Don't be too rough, children," said Mrs. Washburn. "Henry isn't used to such fun."

Dinner that evening was a big steamy ham bone. Bits of cabbage fell from it as one of the children tossed it from the pot to Henry. "What!" thought Henry. "No plate?"

He wondered if he'd ever see a grilled lamb chop again.

By bedtime, Henry was exhausted. His fur-lined basket had been left behind. Where would he sleep?

Just then two of the children carried him off to a room with three bunk beds.

"Henry's sleeping with me!" announced one child, pulling him to one bunk.

"Oh no! Henry's sleeping with me!" protested another, yanking him toward another bunk.

A third child elbowed his way in, and Henry flopped to the floor.

Before he could crawl under one of the beds, a pillow fight broke out.

Thwack! A pillow smacked into Henry's face. He barked. Loud!

Mrs. Washburn came, scurrying down the hallway. The children scattered into their beds.

"Why, Henry!" scolded Mrs. Washburn. "You never barked like that before! Quiet down, or the children will never get to sleep!"

On Sunday, there was no park or classical orchestra. No cool and fragrant grass. Just the Washburn's backyard with its dandelion clumps and creaky swings and a fort made out of empty cardboard boxes.

The children wrestled with Henry. They scratched his ears and tied an old red Christmas ribbon around his neck. They tried to make him chase the cat next door. Baby Washburn even kissed him—a big, sloppy, wet, strawberry-lollipop kiss, right on the nose.

Later, when Baby toppled over onto Henry's tail, they both cried: "Yeeeeoooooooow!"

Mrs. Washburn poked her head out of the back door. "Don't hurt baby, Henry."

Days, weeks, months passed.

Henry learned to put up with pillow fights and strawberry kisses. He learned to ignore the neighbor's cat and to wriggle Christmas ribbons off his neck. He even learned to eat steamy ham bones.

And then one day, everything changed. Just like that. Professor Penrose returned.

The long black limousine came to take Henry back to the professor's fine stone house.

The Washburn children gathered on their front porch. Tears streamed down their cheeks. "Goodbye, Henry," they sniffled sadly. "Goodbye!"

That evening, after being groomed by Miss Fifi (who kept sighing over the tangles in his coat) and after being fed two plump, perfectly grilled lamb chops (in his own monogrammed dish), Henry climbed into his fur-lined basket in front of the fireplace.

He yawned. He laid his head on his front paws. He closed his eyes.

But he did not go to sleep.

Something was wrong. Everything was so quiet, so peaceful. Too quiet. Too peaceful.

Henry climbed out of his basket. He nudged open the front door and headed down the road to the Washburn's house. At first he walked properly, as he had been taught. Then he ran.

When he arrived, he scratched at the door.

Mrs. Washburn opened it. "Why, it's you, Henry. Welcome home!"

Henry dashed up the stairs and into the children's bedroom. It was dark. Thwack! A pillow smacked into his face.

Henry ducked under one of the beds. He smelled the faint scent of strawberry, and as he drifted off to sleep, he was thinking to himself: You have the life, Henry, my boy. You have the life.

2 Your partner retells what he/she has heard. Check if any information is missing in his/her retelling.

3 Tell your partner a story about your pet(s) or the pets and their owners you know about.

Sentence-making

Pick out useful words and expressions from the following sentences and make sentences with them.

Example

Mr. Smith is well known in Washington D.C. **because of** his many social blunders.

  ➢ He was late because of the traffic jam.
  ➢ The little girl became interested in French because of her sister.
  ➢ The students did not do morning exercise because of the rain.

- He received an invitation to a fashionable banquet.
- He spoke to other guests whether he knew them or not.
- I find very little to admire about him.
- Smith continued in spite of her coldness.
- I really can't see how he received his appointment, unless he is perhaps a relative of the president.
- He was the man for the job.
- We're looking for a watch.
- I'm afraid they're far more expensive than this one.
- Would you show us one watch, please?
- What in the world is going on?
- Mrs. Washburn agreed to take Henry to her home until the professor returned.
- Professor Penrose hated to send Henry to live on the other side of the city.
- Henry was deposited in a sea of soap bubbles.
- His fur-lined basket had been left behind.
- Henry learned to put up with pillow fights and strawberry kisses.
- He headed down the road to the Washburn's house.

Scripts

Text A   Do You Know Who I Am?

Mr. Smith is well known in Washington D.C. because of his many social blunders[1]. He always likes to attend the various social functions because he wants to expand his circle of friends[2]. Whenever he is invited, he goes, unless he is ill.

Recently he received an invitation to a fashionable banquet. Although he did not know the hostess, he accepted the invitation. He was secretly very pleased because he felt that his reputation as a desirable guest was growing.

When he arrived at the banquet hall, he found that about one hundred people had been invited. He began to move around the hall. He spoke to other guests whether he knew them or not.[3] He soon realized that he had never met any of the other people present although they seemed to know each other.

At dinner, he was seated beside a very dignified woman[4]. The woman tried to be friendly even though she had never met Mr. Smith before. She spoke politely whenever he spoke to her. Between the first and second course[5] of the meal, she turned to Mr. Smith and said, "Do you see that gray-haired man at the end of the table? The one with the glasses."

"Ah, yes. Who is he?" asked Mr. Smith.

"He's the Secretary of the Interior[6]!" she replied.

Mr. Smith said: "So that's the Secretary of the Interior! I'm afraid that I find very little to admire about him[7], although he is the secretary."

The woman stiffened[8] and did not reply. Smith continued in spite of her coldness. "I really can't see how he received his appointment, unless he is perhaps a relative of the president."

"It hardly matters whether you like the secretary or not," she said. "He was chosen because the president thought he was the man for the job[9]. If he does the job well, you should have no complaint."

"That's just it," persisted Smith. "No one does the things he does, unless he is a complete fool![10]" "Sir!" said the woman in all her dignity. "Do you know who I am?"

"No," replied Smith.

"I am the secretary's wife," she said coldly. Mr. Smith was flabbergasted[11], but he went on in spite of his embarrassment.

"Madam, do you know who I am?"

"No, I don't," the woman replied.

"Thank goodness!" exclaimed Mr. Smith, as he quickly left the table.

Text B   Hands Up!¹²

This was the conversation in an expensive shop in London. A man and a woman walked in and...

Salesman: Can I help you?

Woman: Yes, we're looking for a watch. It's for me.

Salesman: I see. What price are you interested in?

Man: The price doesn't matter. But it must be a gold watch.

Woman: And waterproof. I must have a waterproof watch!

Salesman: Hmm...something like this, perhaps. It's one of our best watches. Made in Switzerland. Fully waterproof. With a calendar and...

Man: It's nice...but haven't you got anything better?

Salesman: Better? Better than this? Well, we have some Orly de luxe watches¹³... probably the best watch in the world. But I'm afraid they're far more expensive than this one. They cost...

Man: Would you show us one, please?

Woman: Yes, could we see one of them, please?

Salesman: They're in the manager's office. You see, we don't...

Man: Could you possibly get one or two of them now?

Salesman: Er...yes, of course. Would you wait here for a moment, please?

He goes to the manager's office and knocks on the door.

Manager: Come in.

Salesman: Mr. Crawford, I have two customers who...

Woman: All right! Hands up! Stand over there!

Salesman: What in the world¹⁴...

Man: Shut up! And open that safe¹⁵! Come on! Open it!

Manager: I...I can't open it.

Man: What do you mean? You must open it.

Manager: You told me to put my hands up. How can I open the safe with my hands up?

Notes

1   social blunders: 社交中的错误

2   expand his circle of friends: 扩大他的朋友圈

3   He spoke to other guests whether he knew them or not.: 不管认识与否，他都与其他客人说话。

4   a very dignified woman: 一位非常高贵的妇人

5   Between the first and second course: 在第一道和第二道菜之间

6   the Secretary of the Interior: 内政部长

7   I find very little to admire about him: 我觉得他没有什么值得我钦佩的

8   The woman stiffened: 这位夫人绷着脸

9   he was the man for the job: 他就是这个职位的合适人选

10   No one does the things he does, unless he is a complete fool!: 一个人如果不是十足的傻瓜的话，他就不会做他（内政部长）做的事情！

11   flabbergasted: 目瞪口呆的

12   Hands Up!: 举起手来!

13   Orly de luxe watches: 奥丽牌高级手表

14   What in the world: 到底……这个句子不完整，可以是 What in the world are you doing?

15   open that safe: 打开那个保险柜

Lesson 29

Text A

My Father's Son

1 **Discuss briefly the questions with your partner.**

Did you ever say "I love you" to your father? Why/Why not?

2 **Listen to Text A once and answer the following questions.**

1   What is the story about?

_____

2   How old was the boy? Was he an outstanding student at school?

_____

3   What was the boy's father?

_____

4   Why did the boy often wonder how his father ever had a son like him?

_____

3 **Listen to Text A again. Take notes and answer the questions below.**

1   What was the boy good at?

_____

2   Where did the boy keep all his poems and stories?

_____

3   What was the boy's dream?

_____

4   What did the boy often daydream about?

_____

5   What did the boy's teacher announce one day?

_____

6   Who donated the prizes?

_____

7   What were the prizes?

_____

8   Why did the boy decide not to begin the essay with "My father is an astronaut"?

_____

9   What did the boy's father do when he had a nightmare?

_____

10   What did the boy's father do when his dog Spotty was killed by a car?

_____

11   What present did the boy's father give him at his eighth birthday party?

_____

12   Why did the boy's father lie to his friends when he cried?

_____

13   What did the boy's father do when his grandpa died?

_____

14   What did the boy find out the next day when he handed in his essay?

_____

15   Did other people expect the boy to win? Why?

_____

16   Was the boy anxious to win? Why not?

_____

17   Who was the third-prize winner?

_____

18   Who was the second-prize winner? How did he feel when he was on the stage? Why? What was the title of his essay?

_____

19   What did the boy do while reading his essay?

_____

20   What did the boy see?

_____

21   What did the boy say to his father when he got back to his seat? Why?

_____

22   What did the boy's father do when he got back to his seat?

_____

23   Was the boy's dream realized? Why?

_____

4 **Retell the story of Text A.**

1　Form a group of three or four and retell the story together. Take turns to give sentences until the story is completed. You may choose one of the following examples as the beginning of your story.

> - I had never expected to win any prize at school. But when my English teacher announced the Father's Day essay contest, I was determined to do my best to impress my father.
> - There was a Father's Day essay contest at my school. To my surprise, I won the second prize.
> - I am an astronaut. I went to a Father's Day essay contest at my son's school. I saw my son going up to the stage.

2　Regroup with students from different groups in step 1. Each student retells the story from his/her previous group.

5 **Discuss the following questions in groups of three or four. After the discussion, select one member of your group to report to the class what you have talked about.**

1　Tell your partner one of the stories between you and your father that impressed you most.

2　What do you think is the ideal relationship between father and son/daughter?

Text B

What's the Matter with You?

1 **Listen to Text B once and answer the following questions.**

1　What is the conversation about?

_____

2　Where does the conversation take place, at the patient's home or in a hospital?

_____

3　Who do you think shows the way for the doctor?

_____

2 **Listen to Text B again. Take notes and answer the questions below.**

1   What does the doctor say to Peter when he sees him?

_____

2   What is wrong with Peter?

_____

3   What did Peter eat yesterday evening?

_____

4   How much ice cream did Peter eat?

_____

5   Does Peter think he had eaten too much? Why?

_____

6   How old do you think Peter could be?

_____

3 **Describe to your partner the picture below with the following words and expressions.**

a patient

sit in bed

offer treatment

a serious case

an acute case

a chronic case

take one's temperature

put a thermometer under the patient's tongue
show one's tongue
feel one's pulse
take one's blood pressure
follow the doctor's orders
call in a doctor for consultation
put on a stethoscope
read the thermometer
wear glasses
in a doctor's overall
wrinkles on one's forehead
a medical kit
receive medical treatment
look concerned
wear a worried look
write out a prescription
a qualified doctor
look weak
take the doctor's advice
have trouble with one's stomach
recover from

4 Suppose you are Dr. Dawes and your partner plays the role of Peter. What would you say to Peter after your checkup? Make a conversation.

Text C

A Miserly Master and a Greedy Servant

1 Read the following text aloud to your partner. Your partner listens to you without looking at the text.

A long time ago, there was a rich old man who loved wine and good food above everything else. And he had a servant who loved drinking and eating as much as his master did.

Each time the rich old man went out, he had to hide his wine and food away. But each time the servant found them and he helped himself to the bottles of wine and all the nice food. Of course, the rich old man knew who did it and was displeased. But he could do nothing about it because he had never caught his servant drinking his wine or eating his food.

One day, the old man was invited to dinner at the home of one of his friends.

He did not know what to do with the wine, meat and chicken he had just bought.

Certainly he could not leave them to the servant. Then he had an idea. He called up the servant and said to him: "I'll be away for the whole evening, and I'll leave you to look after the house. In the cupboard, there are two bottles filled with poison. Be careful about it. You'll be killed if you take even a drop of it. There is also some meat and chicken in the cupboard. Take care of them." With these words the rich old man left home.

As soon as the master turned his back, the servant opened the cupboard and began to enjoy all the nice things in it. He emptied the two bottles and ate up the meat, the chicken and everything else he found in the cupboard. He was satisfied and soon fell asleep.

At midnight, the rich old man returned home. He looked into the cupboard and, to his great surprise, all his wine and food were gone. He was mad with anger and called the servant up.

"Oh, Master," the servant began before the old man could open his mouth. "While you were away, the neighbor's black cat stole into our kitchen and ate up everything in the cupboard. I knew you would be very angry with me. I was so afraid that I drank the two bottles of poison to kill myself." There were even tears in the servant's eyes. "Oh, Master," he continued. "Please don't get angry with a dying man. I'll soon be dead."

The rich old man, of course, did not believe a word of his story. But again, he could do nothing about it.

2 Your partner retells the story to you. Check if any information is missing in his/her retelling.

3 What would you do if you did something inappropriate, to admit it and try to make it right, or to cover it up and find excuses for it? Why?

Sentence-making

Pick out useful words and expressions from the following sentences and make sentences with them.

Example

Everybody **expects you to** be special or perfect.

> My parents expect me to be successful.
> You are expected to finish the work in time.
> He expects us to be at the party this afternoon.

- I mean he's so special and so good at everything he does.
- Well, to tell you the truth, I do have a little talent that nobody knows about.
- But I used to dream about doing something spectacular to impress my father and make him proud of me.
- I remembered how he surprised me with a new puppy at my eighth birthday party.
- David's allergy bothers him a lot this time of year.
- I bet you'll win the contest.
- It was enough just to be my father's son.
- What's the matter with you?
- Show me your tongue.
- I went to a birthday party.
- How many pieces of cake did you eat?
- He helped himself to the bottles of wine and all the nice food.
- He could do nothing about it.
- He had never caught his servant drinking his wine or eating his food.
- I'll leave you to look after the house.

Scripts

Text A   My Father's Son

It's hard being an astronaut's[1] son. I mean, everybody expects you to be special or perfect, and I'm just an average eleven-year-old kid[2]. I'm an average student, and I'm average, too, when it comes to basketball, football, soccer, and baseball.

I often wonder how my father ever had a son like me. I mean he's so special and so good at everything he does. In high school, he was the captain of the football team[3], the class president, and the editor of the school magazine[4].

Well, to tell you the truth[5], I do have a little talent[6] that nobody knows about. I write poems and stories and keep them in a red notebook in my bottom desk drawer[7].

Nowadays I dream about being a famous writer[8], but I used to dream about doing something spectacular[9] to impress my father[10] and make him proud of me— something like rescuing a child from a burning building[11] or chasing a robber away from an old lady[12].

I was daydreaming[13] in school one morning, which I do often. I was daydreaming about being some kind of hero, like discovering an instant cure for cancer[14] or a shot for mental illness[15], when I heard my English teacher announce a Father's Day essay contest[16] for the whole school.

"I hope we have a winner right here in my English class," she said. "The PTA[17] has donated[18] three cash prizes[19]—one hundred dollars for first prize, fifty dollars for second, and twenty-five dollars for third prize."

After school, I walked home, thinking about the essay I would write. "My father is an astronaut," I would start out[20]. No, I decided. I wouldn't do that. The whole country and maybe even the whole world saw my father as an astronaut, but that wasn't the way I saw him[21].

When I got home, I kissed my mom quickly. Then I went upstairs to my room and sat down with a pen and a pad of paper. I started to think about what I would write.

How did I see my father?[22] Hmm.

I saw him sitting with me in the dark[23] when I was a little kid and had a nightmare[24].

I saw him teaching me how to use a bat[25] and how to throw a baseball.

I remembered how he hugged[26] me for hours when my dog Spotty was hit and killed by a car[27].

And I remembered how he surprised me with a new puppy[28] at my eighth birthday party. When I started to cry, he told all the kids that I had a bad allergy[29]. "David's allergy bothers him a lot this time of year," dad said.

And I remembered how he sat and tried to explain death to me when Grandpa Bob died. These were the things I was going to write about my dad. To me, he wasn't just a world-famous astronaut. He was my dad.

I wrote about all these memories and put them in my essay. I handed it in the next day and was surprised to find out that the winning essays[30] would be read in the auditorium[31] on Thursday night. All the parents and students were invited.

My parents and I went to school Thursday night. One of our neighbors said, "I bet[32] you'll win the contest, David. I bet you wrote what it's like to be the son of an astronaut, and you're the only one in town who could write about that."

My dad looked at me, and I shrugged[33]. I hadn't shown him the essay, and now I almost hoped I wouldn't win. I didn't want to win just because my father was an astronaut.

When third prize was announced and it wasn't me, I was relieved and disappointed at the same time[34]. Ellen Gordon won third prize, and she read her essay.

The second-prize winner was announced next. It was me.

I went up to the stage, my knees shaking[35]. I read my essay and wondered if my voice was shaking, too. It was scary[36] standing up in front of all those people. I called my essay "My Father's Son." I watched my parents as I read. When I finished reading, the audience applauded[37]. I saw my father blowing his nose. Tears were running down my mother's face. I went back to my seat.

"I see you have an allergy, too, Dad," I tried to joke.

Dad nodded, cleared his throat, and put his hand on my shoulder[38]. "Son, this is the proudest moment of my life," he said.

It was the proudest moment of my life, too. Maybe I'll never be a great hero or win a Nobel Prize[39], but just then, it was enough just to be my father's son.

Text B　What's the Matter with You?

Mrs. Welsh: Good afternoon, Dr. Dawes.
Dr. Dawes: Good afternoon, Mrs. Welsh.
Mrs. Welsh: Please come this way[40], Doctor. Peter's in this room.
Dr. Dawes: Well, Peter. I'm sorry you're ill. What's the matter with you?
Peter: I don't know, Doctor. I'm ill. I have a headache and a stomachache.[41]
Dr. Dawes: Show me your tongue.[42] What did you eat yesterday?
Peter: Well, Doctor, I...
Dr. Dawes: Did you eat any cake?
Peter: Yes, I ate some cake.

Dr. Dawes: Did you eat any ice cream?

Peter: Well, yes, I did. I ate some ice cream.

Dr. Dawes: Did you eat any candy[43]?

Peter: Well, yes, I did. I ate some candy.

Dr. Dawes: Young man, tell me everything you ate yesterday evening.

Peter: Well, Doctor. I went to a birthday party.

Dr. Dawes: I see! How many pieces of cake[44] did you eat?

Peter: Three, Doctor.

Dr. Dawes: How many plates of ice cream[45] did you eat, young man?

Peter: Gosh[46], Doctor. I had only three plates of ice cream. John had four.

Notes

1   an astronaut: 一名宇航员

2   an average eleven-year-old kid: 一个普通的十一岁孩子

3   the captain of the football team: 橄榄球队长，在美语中，football 是橄榄球，soccer 是足球

4   the editor of the school magazine: 校刊的编辑

5   tell you the truth: 实话对你讲

6   talent: 才能

7   in my bottom desk drawer: 在我书桌最下层的抽屉里

8   dream about being a famous writer: 梦想成为著名的作家

9   spectacular: 惊人的

10   impress my father: 给我父亲留下深刻印象

11   rescuing a child from a burning building: 从烈火燃烧的大楼中救出一个小孩

12   chasing a robber away from an old lady: 把抢劫老太太的强盗赶走

13   daydreaming: 做白日梦

14   an instant cure for cancer: 速效治癌药

15   a shot for mental illness: 治精神病的针剂

16   announce a Father's Day essay contest: 宣布父亲节作文比赛

17   The PTA (Parent-Teacher Association): 家长与教师协会

18   donated: 捐赠

19   three cash prizes: 三个现金奖项

20   start out: 起头，开始

21   but that wasn't the way I saw him: 但我并不是那样看他的

22   How did I see my father?: 我怎么看我父亲?

23   in the dark: 黑暗中

24   a nightmare: 一场噩梦

25   a bat: （棒球运动中用的）球棒

26   hugged: 拥抱

27   when my dog Spotty was hit and killed by a car: 当我的狗斯波蒂被汽车撞死后

28   a new puppy: 一只新的小狗

29   I had a bad allergy: 我过敏很严重

30   the winning essays: 获奖作文

31   in the auditorium: 在礼堂

32   I bet: 我断定，我敢说

33   shrugged: 耸肩

34   I was relieved and disappointed at the same time: 我松了一口气，同时又有些失望

35   my knees shaking: 我的膝盖发抖

36   scary: 害怕的

37   applauded: 鼓掌

38   put his hand on my shoulder: 把他的手放在我的肩上

39   a Nobel Prize: 诺贝尔奖

40   come this way: 这边走

41   I have a headache and a stomachache.: 我头痛、肚子痛。

42   Show me your tongue.: 让我看看你的舌头。

43   candy: 糖果，美国用法，英国人一般用 sweet

44   How many pieces of cake: 多少块蛋糕

45   How many plates of ice cream: 多少碟冰激凌

46   Gosh: 啊呀，表示惊讶

Lesson 30

Text A

Learn to Eat like a Grown-up.

1 **Discuss briefly the questions with your partner.**

Did you ever learn table manners when you were a child? Share with your partner the Chinese table manners you know.

2 **Listen to Text A once and answer the following questions.**

1 What is the conversation about?

_____

2 How many people are there in the conversation?

_____

3 What are they going to do?

_____

3 **Listen to Text A again. Take notes and answer the questions below.**

1 Does Chris feel hungry?

_____

2 What does Chris' mother think he must learn since he is getting to be a big boy?

_____

3 What does Chris think growing up means?

_____

4 What is the little plate for?

_____

5 How does mustard taste?

_____

6 What does Chris' father say about his sitting posture at the table?

_____

7　Why does Chris prefer to eat elsewhere?

_____

8　Why isn't Chris allowed to put his knife into his mouth?

_____

9　Why doesn't Chris want to use his fork?

_____

10　How does Chris' mother say he should lay his knife and fork when he's finished with the main course?

_____

11　What is supposed to be used more when it comes to the sweets?

_____

12　When is the spoon to be used?

_____

13　What does Chris' mother tell him to say when he wants something at the table?

_____

4　Retell the story of Text A.

1　Form a group of three or four and retell the story together. Take turns to give sentences until the story is completed. You may choose one of the following examples as the beginning of your story.

> - I was seated at the dining table and felt quite hungry. But my mother said I was getting to be a big boy and must learn to eat like a grown-up.
> - As I glanced at the meal spread before me, I knew it was the perfect opportunity to teach my son table manners.
> - Today, I am determined to teach my son table manners. I set the table beautifully and call my husband and son to have the meal.

2　Regroup with students from different groups in step 1. Each student retells the story from his/her previous group.

5　Discuss the following questions in groups of three or four. After the discussion, select one member of your group to report to the class what you have talked about.

1　What do you know about the do's and don'ts at a Western dinner table?

2　Do you think Chris' parents are too strict with him? How did your parents teach you the table manners when you were a child?

Text B

A Quiz on General Knowledge

1 **Listen to Text B once and answer the following questions.**

1   What is the conversation about?

_____

2   How many people are involved in the conversation?

_____

3   What are they doing?

_____

_____

2 **Listen to Text B again. Take notes and answer the questions below.**

1   Does Tony know when America was discovered?

_____

2   Who actually discovered America? And when?

_____

3   Does Tony agree with Charles' answer?

_____

4   Who does Tony think traveled to America before Columbus?

_____

5   Who else does Tony mention?

_____

6   What did Edison invent according to the conversation?

_____

7   What is Tony's harder question?

_____

8   Can Charles answer Tony's question?

_____

9   What is Charles' guess?

_____

10   What is Charles' last question?

_____

11   Does Tony think Charles' question is difficult?

_____

12   Does Tony know the answer?

_____

3 Describe to your partner the picture below with the following words and expressions.

a small boat

look like a dragon boat

sail on the ocean

on an expedition to

wear costumes

be beautifully decorated

rove from one place to another

carry a spear

set out

hoist the sails

the mainmast

stand on the deck

row a boat

at the port

a tent on the stern

a cloudy day

be covered with dark clouds

a calm sea

come across hardships and difficulties

on the voyage to

4 You and your partner go on with the game Charles and Tony have been playing by asking each other questions about general knowledge.

Text C

Good Manners

1 Read the following text aloud to your partner. Your partner listens to you without looking at the text.

> We say that a person has good manners if he or she behaves politely and is kind and helpful to others. Everyone likes a person with good manners but no one likes a person with bad manners. "Yes," you may say, "but what are good manners? How does one know what to do and what not to do?"
>
> Well, here are some examples of the things that a well-mannered person does or does not do.
>
> He never laughs at people when they are in trouble. Instead, he tries to help them. He is always kind, never cruel, to people. When people are waiting for a bus, or in a bank, he takes his turn. He does not push to the front line of the queue. In the bus, he gives his seat to an older person or a lady who is standing. If he accidentally bumps into someone, or gets in their way, he says "Excuse me" or "I'm sorry."
>
> He says "Please" when he makes a request, and "Thank you" when he receives something. He stands up when he is speaking to a lady or an older person, and he does not sit down until the other person is seated. He does not interrupt other people when they are talking. He does not talk too much himself. He does not talk loudly or laugh loudly in public. When he is eating, he does not speak with his mouth full of food. He uses a tissue when he sneezes or coughs.

2 Your partner retells the story to you. Check if any information is missing in his/her retelling.

3 Discuss with your partner the proper manners for a formal banquet and a party at a friend's house respectively.

Sentence-making

Pick out useful words and expressions from the following sentences and make sentences with them.

Example

I'm ready.
So am I.

⁣⁣ ▷ He went to school yesterday.

So did I.

▷ She is going to write her paper in the library.

So is Tom.

▷ I have finished my homework.

So have your classmates.

- Help yourself to vegetables from the dish.
- Don't make a noise when you are eating.
- I think it would be better if I took my plate away to the nursery.
- Leave the lad alone.
- There seems to be a great deal to learn.
- May I have some more pudding?
- You mustn't expect me to learn everything at once.
- In a way, that's right.
- Everyone likes a person with good manners.
- When people are waiting for a bus, he takes his turn.
- He says "Please" when he makes a request.
- He does not sit down until the other person is seated.

Scripts

Text A   Learn to Eat like a Grown-up.

Mother: The table's laid. Come along, both of you, and let us begin.

Father: I'm ready. I feel quite hungry.

Chris: So am I. I could eat a horse.[1]

Mother: Well, we haven't got a horse for you, but what we have got is quite nice. Sit there and see how well you can behave. Remember, you're getting to be a big boy and you must learn to eat like a grown-up.

Chris: Does that mean that I can eat more?

Mother: We want you to have a good meal, though we don't want you to stuff yourself[2]. Your place has been laid just like ours.

Chris: What's this little plate for?

Mother: That's for your bread. Most people eat a little bread with their meat and vegetables.

Chris: Mother, aren't you going to cut my meat up for me any more?

Mother: No, I'm not. We have put a knife and fork for you and you must learn how to use them. Here is your meat. Help yourself to vegetables from the dish. Don't take more than you can eat.[3]

Chris: All right, Mother. May I take some mustard[4]?

Father: You may, but I don't think you'll like it. You'll find it hot. Now sit up properly. Don't lean back and don't lean too far forward.

Mother: And take your elbows off the tablecloth.

Father: And don't take too much on your fork[5]. You shouldn't open your mouth wide at meals.

Mother: Don't make a noise when you are eating.

Chris: Good gracious! I think it would be better if I took my plate away to the nursery. I shan't be able to eat at all if I try to remember all those things.

Father: Stay where you are.[6] You'll soon learn.

Chris begins to eat. He puts some vegetables into his mouth with his knife.

Mother: What are you doing? Don't you know that you must never put your knife into your mouth?

Chris: But why, Mummy? It's easier like that sometimes.

Father: You might cut your mouth. Do you want to make your mouth bigger than it is? Use your fork.

Chris: No, I don't. But I might prick my tongue with the points of my fork[7].

Father: Well, you must learn not to.

Mother: There, leave the lad alone.[8] He'll soon learn. Have you finished, dear? Lay your knife and fork on your plate. No, don't cross them. Put the handles toward you.

Father: Now, here come the sweets. Here's your plate. Use that spoon and fork. Use your fork more than your spoon.

Chris: But why? Isn't it polite to use the spoon?

Mother: Of course, it is, but most people use the fork more than the spoon. Use the spoon when you have to.

Chris: You mean for eating very soft stuff?

Mother: That's right. Why haven't you drunk any water?[9]

Chris drinks some water and puts his glass down on the left of his plate.

Father: Not there. On your right.

Chris: But why?

Father: Because it is nearer to your right hand. It's handier there.

Chris: All right, Dad. There seems to be a great deal to learn. Give me some more pudding, Mother.

Mother: "Give me" doesn't get.[10] Say "May I have…?"

Chris: May I have some more pudding?

Mother: Here you are. What's that I see? Dirty hands? Don't come to the table with dirty hands again.[11]

Father: And brush your hair next time you come.

Chris: I'll try to remember. But you mustn't expect me to learn everything at once. May I get down now?

Mother: Very well. Run along.

Text B   A Quiz on General Knowledge[12]

Charles Kent and Tony Smith are playing a game. They are asking each other questions about general knowledge.

Charles: When was America discovered, Tony?

Tony: I'm not certain. Do you know?

Charles: America was discovered by Christopher Columbus[13] in 1492.

Tony: In a way, that's right. But the Vikings traveled there long before Columbus. And what about Native Americans[14]?

Charles: All right. Ask me a question now.

Tony: Who invented the electric light bulb?

Charles: That's easy. It was invented by Edison[15].

Tony: Correct. Now for a harder question. Who will be the first man on Mars?

Charles: I can't answer that. But I think Mars will be visited by men before the end
             of this century.

Tony: Ask me a question now.

Charles: All right. What is the nearest planet to the sun?

Tony: That's easy. It's...er...Venus[16]. No. Pluto[17]. No. Wait a minute. It's on the tip
             of my tongue.[18] Oh dear, what is the nearest planet to the sun?

Notes

1   I could eat a horse.: 我可以吃掉一匹马，意思是能吃很多。

2   we don't want you to stuff yourself: 我们不想你吃撑了

3   Don't take more than you can eat.: 吃多少取多少。

4   mustard: 芥末

5   don't take too much on your fork: 不要用叉子叉太多

6   Stay where you are.: 你就在那儿坐着，别动。

7   I might prick my tongue with the points of my fork: 叉子尖会叉到我的舌头

8   There, leave the lad alone.: 得了，别说孩子了。There 作感叹词。

9   Why haven't you drunk any water?: 你为什么没喝水啊？

10   "Give me" doesn't get.: 说"给我"要不来东西。

11   Don't come to the table with dirty hands again.: 下次不许脏着手来吃饭。

12   General Knowledge: 常识

13   Christopher Columbus: 克里斯托弗·哥伦布，意大利航海家

14   Native Americans: 印第安人

15   Edison: 爱迪生，即 Thomas A. Edison，美国发明家

16   Venus: 金星

17   Pluto: 冥王星

18   It's on the tip of my tongue.: 就在我嘴边，意思是记得某件事，但一时说不出来。